BILLY FITZGERALD

PRIMATE

An *authorized portrait*
of
Cardinal Cahal B. Daly

Fount
An Imprint of HarperCollins*Publishers*

Fount Paperbacks is an imprint of
HarperCollins*Religious*
Part of HarperCollins*Publishers*
77–85 Fulham Palace Road, London W6 8JB

First published in Great Britain
in 1992 by Fount Paperbacks

1 3 5 7 9 10 8 6 4 2

A catalogue record for this book is
available from the British Library

ISBN 0 00 627602 4

Typeset by Medcalf Type Ltd, Bicester, Oxon

Printed and bound in Great Britain by
HarperCollinsManufacturing Glasgow

*Dedicated to the memory of
my sister, Ann (Sister Sou, IBVM),
who in her short life
did so much in the fields of
education and ecumenics
in Ireland both north and south*

Table of Contents

Preface

ONE SUNNY DAY in 1979 a television documentary crew
from Radio Telefis Eireann, the Irish national broadcasting service, were setting up their equipment in the town
square of Castel Gandolfo, the mountain village outside Rome
where the Roman Pontiffs, traditionally, have retired from the
scorching heat of the Roman summer, to the *palazzo* which
was once the summer villa of the Barberini family. The TV
crew were there as part of the run-up to the recently announced
papal visit to Ireland, due to take place at the end of that
September. As the television crew watched, they saw a small
car draw up in the town carpark and a slight figure, dressed
in clerical black and carrying a briefcase, stepped out and swiftly
walked up to the papal *palazzo*, scarcely noticed by anyone
in the square. The Swiss Guard on duty at the portal gave
a quiet salute, and the diminutive figure disappeared inside.
It was Bishop Cahal Daly of the Irish diocese of Ardagh and
Clonmacnoise.

Rumour and press speculation had suggested that the Irish
Bishops' Conference had delegated Bishop Daly to be the
liaison man between themselves and the Pope. His task would
be to brief the Pontiff on the complexities of the Irish political
situation and, it was said by some, even to help the Pope to

draft the speeches which he would deliver in the course of his Irish visit. This was something which the bishop refused ever afterwards either to confirm or deny. But it is certain that he was a special visitor to Castel Gandolfo in those summer days of 1979. He would have become well known by the Holy Father who, many years later, would be looking for someone to become Archbishop of Armagh, Ireland's primatial See . . .

Who knows a bishop? Bishops are private people who have been thrust into public office. This almost inevitably means that bishops are known, when known at all, in their public persona. It could be thought of as part of his vocation that a bishop has to struggle to be known and understood, both by his clergy and by his flock at large. This is not easy. Bishops are fair game for a persistent press. Their every publicly expressed thought or word is liable to selective quotation. "Bishop slams politician" or "Bishop in controversy" are the very currency of popular journalism. And yet, behind every such headline there is a real person, struggling to cope with what may, at times, seem to be a well-nigh impossible job.

The office of bishop as we in the Western Church know it has been the subject of continuous development. That there were bishops in the early Church is undeniable. They partake in the three-fold sacrament of Orders as defined in the Roman Catholic Church. That those bishops of the primitive Church, if they were to come back into the twentieth-century Church, would recognize their successors in their modern ministry is at least debatable. The primary task of preaching the Gospel and administering the Sacraments of course remains the same, but so much else, the peripherals, have altered out of all recognition.

Those with the best chance of getting to know their bishop are probably the diocesan clergy. He is their "managing director", to use the modern term. They are his "reps" out on the ground of the diocese. At best, a bishop will be seen by the people of any given parish on those annual or even biennial occasions when he visits them to administer the Sacrament of Confirmation to their children. The insistent and at times almost overwhelming burden of administration keeps him apart from his flock for much of his time.

If all this is true of any diocesan bishop, how much more so of a primate. Primacy brings with it precious few perks, but many additional burdens. In addition to all the normal duties of a diocesan bishop, a primate normally presides over the assembled bishops of his country, the Episcopal Conference. His responsibilities are national as well as diocesan. The danger, of course, is that he becomes more and more distant, known to the ordinary people of God as a remote figure, glimpsed from time to time on television or in person on ceremonial occasions.

Hence the purpose of this book. With the agreement and generous cooperation of Ireland's latest primate, his family and friends, I hope to be able to bring readers behind the scenes to meet the man behind the office; the no more than mortal man who has accepted the burden of primacy from the hands of Pope John Paul II, at a stage when many another has gratefully accepted retirement from the pressures of work.

I am particularly grateful to the primate for the generous way in which he made both himself and his archives available to me. Much of the material in this book is, therefore, his. Any errors or omissions, on the other hand, are totally my own!

My thanks must also go to Moira Reilly of HarperCollins whose charisms are of encouragement and support.

Billy FitzGerald
September 1991

CHAPTER ONE

A New Beginning

My son, if you aspire to serve the Lord
prepare yourself for an ordeal.
Be sincere of heart, be steadfast,
and do not be alarmed
when disaster comes.

[ECCLESIASTICUS 2:1–2]

SUNDAY, DECEMBER 16th, 1990. The main road from Dublin to the North of Ireland was closed all day. A suspected IRA booby-trap bomb was thought to be in a truck, abandoned during the night at the Killeen border crossing-point. As a result, all north-bound traffic had to make its way via the rather more tortuous inland route through Castleblayney and Monaghan. And there was more traffic than usual that day, for at three o'clock in the afternoon, the Most Reverend Cahal Brendan Daly, formerly Bishop of Down and Connor and of Ardagh and Clonmacnoise, was to be installed as Archbishop of Armagh, and Primate of All Ireland, the 114th successor to Saint Patrick.

When Patrick himself chose Ard Macha to be the site of his principal church, its origins were already lost in the damp mists of Irish prehistory. It had been the seat of the chieftains of the historic Fifth of Ulster who, in naming it, had given honour to their pagan goddess, Macha.

By the fifth century at least, the church at Ard Macha had become, in the style of the time, largely monastic in character; the offices of bishop and abbot being held by one and the same person, and the ecclesiastical community being organized along monastic lines.

From at least the eighth century onwards, the abbots of Armagh, by reason of the historic link of their church to Patrick, were claiming to be primates over the whole Irish Church. The devastation of the Viking invasions in the ninth and tenth centuries proved a hiatus from which the monastery and its school emerged more glorious than before. Now it was proclaimed that none but alumni of Armagh could be appointed masters of studies in any other Irish monastic school. In the year 1004, the High King, Brian Boru himself, declared the supremacy of the church of Armagh. The historic tug-of-power between the diocesan and abbatial systems continued sporadically until The Synod of Kells, in the year 1152, at which the pallium, the specific vestment of an archbishop, was bestowed by the Papal Legate, Cardinal Paparo, on Gilla Mac Liag, former Abbot of Derry, and Armagh had its first canonical archbishop.

The mists of time yielded, in December 1990, to altogether more palpable mists. A combination of near-freezing rain and patchy fog imposed its own speed-limit on the cars heading north, among them the Mercedes carrying the recently-elected President of Ireland, Mary Robinson. The other limousines of the diplomatic corps and other VIPs who, had the weather been kinder, would have journeyed in less time and probably less comfort in the helicopters now grounded in the Republic, mingled with the less illustrious in the tortuous procession northward.

Roadworks just north of the border occasioned a further delay with vehicles taking turns at the temporary traffic-lights controlling a one-way system. (The contractor's name, stencilled large on some of the equipment, read "Crozier"!) And, lest it should have slipped anyone's mind that they were en route to a religious occasion, a little further on, a crudely lettered sign, nailed to a telegraph pole, urged the passers-by: "Prepare to meet thy God".

The scene that greeted the travellers arriving on the hill of Armagh that afternoon could not have been bettered by the great Italian film director Fellini himself. The thickening fog enshrouded the twin spires of the cathedral. By three o'clock, the afternoon light was already fading fast. High on a metal gantry, outside the west door of the cathedral, the television lights cast a metallic-blue light over the whole scene. Scouts and Guides in the guard of honour shivered and stamped their feet on the wet tarmac, ceremonial discipline giving way to the demands of circulation. The procession of acolytes and clergy, forming up on the roadway to the side of the building, and deprived by the fog of any apparent physical setting, seemed poised on the edge of the galaxy; by now, the thickening fog had obscured the TV scaffolding and everything else solid round about. The arc lights, looming haloed through the mist, seemed to hover, unsupported in the air, a pair of alien suns floating in on the scene from another part of the universe.

There was fog inside the cathedral too. It swirled high above the television lights and above the heads of the already assembled congregation, almost obscuring the soaring Gothic arches and reducing the colours of the stained glass windows to a dull grey. From the organ gallery, high above the west door, the sound of Durufle's "Variations on the Veni Creator" gently penetrated the damp air.

Slowly, the cross-bearer led the procession of clergy into the cathedral and up the nave to their places in the sanctuary and the apse, the black and white choir dress of the clergy giving way in turn to the purple of prelates and eventually to the all-white mitres and chasubles of the concelebrating bishops. They were followed by the vivid scarlet of the visiting Cardinals, Etchegaray of the Vatican's Council for Justice and Peace, Cardinal Basil Hume of Westminster and Cardinal Bernard Law of Boston, who took their places in the sanctuary, close to the altar. Above their heads hung, unreached by the television lighting, and barely swaying in the draught from the open doors, the red hats of previous Cardinal Primates of Armagh, Logue, O'Donnell, McRory, Dalton and Conway.

Assembled in the foremost seats of the nave were Mr Peter Brooke, the North of Ireland Secretary, Mr Charles Haughey, *Taoiseach* of the Irish Republic, and Archbishop Robin Eames, Anglican Primate of All Ireland who, together with his colleagues, Archbishop Donald Caird of Dublin and Bishop David Sheppard of Liverpool, headed up the largest assembly of non-Roman Catholic religious leaders ever to have graced such an occasion. Members of the diplomatic corps and governments from near and far all bore witness, by their presence, to the importance of the occasion.

Present too were the new Archbishop's immediate family, Dr Nicholas Daly, from Oxford, Mr Patrick Daly, a retired teacher, and his sisters, Sheila and Rosaleen.

A movement at the main door caused a momentary turning of heads. Then the congregation rose to its feet and in an unprecedented, spontaneous gesture, burst into applause as Ireland's young President, Mary Robinson, on her first official visit north of the border, and dressed for the occasion in a tweed suit of something approaching episcopal purple, walked, accompanied by her husband, Nick, to her priedieu before the sanctuary.

At nine minutes past three exactly, Monsignor Francis MacLarnon, on whose shoulders the administration of the Archdiocese of Armagh had rested during the previous six months, since the sudden death of Cardinal Tomas O Fiaich in Lourdes the previous May, stepped forward at the great west door to greet the new archbishop as he ceremonially crossed the threshold of his cathedral for the first time. With him, in their robes of purple and capes of white sheepskin, the canons of the cathedral chapter echoed his words of welcome. After a blessing with holy water, the procession made its way up the nave to the sanctuary.

A young deacon, the Reverend John Gates, stepped forward to a lectern and read out an English translation of the letter from Pope John Paul II appointing the new archbishop to the see of Armagh. This letter was then presented to Dean MacLarnon for consignment to the diocesan archives. The dean then escorted the archbishop to his presidential chair, the *cathedra*, where he was presented with his crozier and a book of the gospels. From that moment, Armagh had its new archbishop and primate.

"I exult for joy in the Lord, my soul rejoices in my God, for he has clothed me in the garments of salvation, he has wrapped me in the cloak of integrity . . . For as the earth makes fresh things grow, as a garden makes seeds spring up, so will the Lord make both integrity and praise spring up in the sight of the nations." The words of the prophet Isaiah, in the first reading of the Mass, were followed by the words of Saint John's gospel: "I am . . . a voice that cries in the wilderness: make a straight way for the Lord." Then the packed congregation waited to hear the first address of the new primate from the ambo of his new cathedral.

His words were of joy: "It is with joyful hope that I join with you in saying 'yes' to God for the future we shall share together in Armagh. So today is a day of spiritual joy. It is with joy in our hearts today that we draw living water from the wellsprings of our salvation in this holy Eucharist. It is appropriate that my installation should take place on this Third Sunday of Advent. This Sunday is called, in our liturgy, 'Gaudate Sunday'. It takes this name from the first words of the entrance hymn, 'Gaudate'. 'Rejoice'. 'Rejoice in the Lord always,' says Saint Paul, 'again I say rejoice. The Lord is very near.' "

In a homily that sprang from a sensitive awareness of the

many problems both in Armagh and in the lives of men and women throughout the length and breadth of the land, he went on: "There are some, alas, in our society who do not seem to find joy in their faith. They seem to find the Church and its teaching negative and burdensome, as if it denied them space and fulfilment and freedom. That perception could only come from a caricature of what the Church is and teaches. We pastors too, who are such inadequate ministers of the Gospel, must take some of the blame. Certainly, none of the blame lies with Christ or with his Gospel."

In offering his vision of a new Ireland, the archbishop said: "There is a sense of newness in the air in our country at this time. There is an intimation of a new future, of new possibilities and of new beginnings. But all these words are remarkably like the opening lines of the four gospels. Saint Mark begins on a note of almost breathless excitement: 'The beginning of the Good News about Jesus Christ the Son of God'. Now is the opportunity for the Church in Ireland to rediscover that sense of excitement about the Good News of Jesus Christ . . ."

And then a word of caution: "Can we genuinely speak of 'national recovery', while so many citizens of the nation are excluded from that recovery? Wealth does not 'trickle down' automatically to those at the bottom of the heap. A rising economic tide does not 'lift all boats', but leaves many stuck hopelessly and helplessly in the mudflats of poverty . . . No government and no section of society can be satisfied with our record of recovery while unemployment remains so high, emigration continues at unacceptable levels, and real poverty is still the fate of many."

Then, in words addressed particularly to those leaders of other Churches whom he had warmly welcomed at the beginning of the ceremony he said: "Here in this land of ours the ecumenical imperative is particularly pressing. It is sometimes suggested that the momentum has gone out of the ecumenical movement and that ecumenism is reduced again to merely cosmetic gestures. This is not true. Ecumenism is as much as ever in the mainstream of the Church's concerns. But we must make this more visible, until the conviction becomes universally established among the whole people of God that one cannot be authentically Catholic without the ecumenical spirit."

"I have been immeasurably heartened since my appointment by the multitude of messages I have received from church leaders, clergy, lay men and women in the Protestant churches, and by their promises of prayer and support. The large number of Protestant church leaders and clergy and people present with us in this cathedral today touches me deeply. It brings forcefully home to me my duty as bishop to do all in my power to build on this goodwill and to explore with my brothers and sisters in other Churches all opportunities for Catholics and Protestants to work together for mutual understanding and respect, for the removal of reciprocal prejudices and for their replacement by reconciliation and Christian love."

And finally, the archbishop, as so often before in other places and at other times, spoke to those who even to that day would seek to solve their problems and the problems of the nation by violence: "There are people in both communities who keep blindfolds over their consciences which prevent them from seeing the moral enormity of their deeds of violence . . . I appeal to these people, in God's name, to turn to Christ the Lord and to learn from him the meaning of true justice and the way to a just peace. I appeal to them to learn from Christ that love is the secret weapon of the only revolution that really works . . . I appeal particularly to republican activists, who were brought up in their childhood to listen to God and to the Church and who might be expected to listen to a Catholic bishop . . . If or when you call off your campaign, your aims and objectives become in principle attainable through the only means by which they ever could be attained, namely through peaceful political processes. You have no sane reason or justification, moral, rational or political for continuing with your campaign of violence. You have every reason, moral, rational and political, for calling off your campaign now. May Christ, who enlightens every man and woman coming into this world, enlighten your minds and your consciences, so that in his light you may, as Saint Patrick puts it, 'recover your senses for God'."

It was an address which could have left little doubt in the minds of his hearers as to what were to be the priorities on the agenda of the new archbishop in the years to come.

The celebration of the Eucharist which followed was a continuation and heartfelt extension of his prayer for peace. And when, at the Sign of Peace, Archbishop Daly strode to the Presidential priedieu and, smiling, grasped both hands of the President of Ireland, the lenses of the assembled press captured a moment of warmth which was carried, next day, by the papers in Ireland and much further afield.

CHAPTER TWO

A Childhood
in the Glens

Children, listen to me, your father.
Do what I tell you and be safe.
For the Lord honours the father in his children
and upholds the rights of a mother over her sons.
Whoever respects his father atones for his sins,
he who honours his mother is like one amassing a fortune.

[ECCLESIASTICUS 3:1–5]

THE PARENTS OF CAHAL BRENDAN DALY were married in the church of Loughguile, County Antrim, on Christmas Day 1912. There seems to be no family memory of a reason as to why such an unusual day for a wedding had been chosen. But married on Christmas Day they were.

Born in County Roscommon, at Keadue, near Boyle, Charles Daly had trained as a teacher under the De La Salle Brothers, in Waterford, graduating in 1903, and taking charge of his first school, at Corkey, one of the schools in the County Antrim parish of Loughguile, where he lived in rented bachelor quarters.

In Loughguile he met Susan Connolly, a young monitoress, that is, a young woman who had been picked out by her own teachers as being of exceptional talent, and was therefore "kept on" after her own schooling had been completed, as an unpaid trainee-teacher.

Not the least of his problems was that of learning to hear and understand her rapidly-spoken and, initially at any rate, almost, to his southern ears, unintelligible accent of the Glens. It left him, as he said himself, "lost and bewildered"! Not, it would seem, however, that this remained a problem for long. (It was one which bedevelled his initial efforts with the pupils

in his school also!) Nevertheless it did not hinder courtship
and in due course the young couple were married in the church
of Loughguile on that Christmas day of 1912. In the following
years they were blessed with a large family, seven children, of
which five survived infancy.

The living was not easy. In those days, at the beginning of
the century, to be a Catholic in Ireland was to be a second-
class citizen. As elsewhere, the homesteads of Loughguile were,
for the most part, the property of the Protestant ascendancy,
some of whom, it must be admitted, carried on the inherited
attitudes of their planter forebears, dealing with their (largely
Catholic) tenants in ways that were neither charitable not just.
This was not always the case, however, and on at least one
occasion the instructions of the then IRA Command, to
assassinate one of the local landlords, was quite simply refused
for the reason that he was recognized by the people of
Loughguile to be a kindly and compassionate employer who
took good care of all his tenants, irrespective of their religion
or politics.

The "Troubles" which afflicted the whole of Ireland at that
time were brought very close to home for the young
schoolmaster and his family on one occasion. They were living
as tenants in a summer cottage which belonged to a Belfast
wine and spirit merchant by the name of McKeown. The house
had a stable yard, around which there were a number of
outhouses which had been recently renovated and occupied
as a temporary billet by part of the local garrison who had
been bombed out of their barracks by the IRA. Not satisfied
with having destroyed the barracks, the "Boys" decided to
follow up the operation by burning down the new billets. The
fact that the young schoolmaster and his family were
neighbours did not deter them. In fact it meant that the
incendiarists would have easy, intimidatory access to a handy
place to start the fire. Later in his life, Cahal Daly still has

a vivid memory of what happened: He remembers waking up in his cot, in the upstairs nursery and seeing a tall, young man stooping over him and carrying him gently, still in his pyjamas, down the stairs and placing him in his father's arms. The young man, a mere fifteen-year-old, had been "bought" at a hiring-fair in Galway and brought to Antrim to work as a farm hand earlier that year and had been speedily recruited into the IRA. The young Cahal remembers seeing him return into the house and soon he could see flames reaching through the roof of the family home. He remembers his childhood puzzlement; he asked his father, "Why have they brought the dining-room fire up to the roof?" According to plan, the flames quickly spread and the billet of the soldiers, next door, was destroyed. So was the home of the Daly family, together with virtually all their worldly goods.

They moved that night to the home of an aunt on the Connolly side of the family, Auntie Jane Macilhone, in the townland of Tully, who made them welcome and with whom they stayed until schoolmaster Daly was able to find a new cottage to rent nearby.

Many years later, a twist of fate was to stir memories of that night. In the early nineteen-seventies, while on a business visit to Dublin from his diocese of Ardagh and Clonmacnoise, Bishop Daly was in Wynn's Hotel, described in one of Joseph Tomelty's plays as "a great hang-out of priests", as so it was. As he was taking his light pre-meeting lunch, alone, a tall elderly man approached his table. "Excuse me, Father, but would you be Bishop Daly?" "Yes, I am." "Well," said the old man, "we have met before, a long time ago." He turned out to be that young IRA recruit who, all those years ago, had snatched him from sleep to place him in the safe embrace of his father. He himself, at the time of the Treaty, had forsaken his membership of the IRA and returned to his native Galway where he lived out the rest of his life. After a brief discussion in which the two traced for one another the course of their subsequent lives, they shook hands, the older man to return to the obscurity from which he had briefly emerged, the bishop to continue with the ministry for which, Wesley-like, he had been "a brand, snatched from the burning". The two never met again.

Those were the days of the great recession. Most households would have kept a subsistence-level stock of a handful of hens and pigs with the staples, bread and butter, being made by the housewife at home. Even the income of a schoolteacher would have been augmented by such small produce.

Despite her preoccupation with the care of her ever increasing family, Susan Daly, being an energetic and compassionate woman, was ever at the disposal of her neighbours. She constantly was to be seen on her bicycle, visiting the sick of the parish or doing little errands for others less able than herself. She became known as one on whom people could rely. Although she lacked any nursing or medical training, she assumed, or perhaps better, had thrust upon her, the role of an unofficial district nurse, soothing the ills of others and even attending at confinements.

In the early decades of the century, the Glens of Antrim saw a decimation of its population through what has been called the cancer of emigration. Whole families, whose breadwinners could find no work, would put up the shutters on the family home and depart, without even waiting to put the homesteads on the market; there were no prospective buyers. Even here, the skills of Susan Daly were in demand as a letter-writer. Through her pen she kept up contact between the parish of Loughguile and those of its children who suffered in the "scattering".

The atmosphere could hardly have been described as encouraging. Young schoolmaster Daly was teaching children whose future was desperately uncertain. Half of the children in his classroom on any day were destined to be swept away to Canada or New Zealand before ever their education could be completed.

A Father MacDonald, from Scotland, advertised for Irish Catholics to help found a new settlement which came to be known as "The MacDonald Project" in Alberta, Canada. The Macaleese family, near-by neighbours of the Dalys, attracted by such prospects, were quickly away to Canada. Another family, also near neighbours, to New Zealand. The "scattering" was a reality, close to hand.

In a very short time, the population of Loughguile was halved. Nevertheless, a firm grip on the realities of life, combined with a positive attitude to things in general and a solid faith in his own abilities as a teacher enabled Charles Daly to establish a happy home and a firmly-rooted family.

The young Cahal Daly's first experience of school was not a happy one. His older brother, Nicholas, recalls that while he, Cahal, was still too young to be a pupil, he was brought one day to the school for the annual ceremony of the taking of the school photograph. The infant Cahal was to be seen in the centre of the picture, held still by his father, and howling his head off!

Eventually, however, young Cahal Daly attended classes in his own father's school as soon as he was old enough to do so. The schoolmaster's son found little difficulty with his lessons. A certain inherited aptitude was, in later years, to develop into an avid hunger for reading.

Lessons in Loughguile were not, however, all smooth going. There were interruptions, such as were normal in every country townland at the time; youngsters were allowed to stay away from school on those days when the local farmers needed a *meithal* or team of volunteers for harvesting or threshing. There is extant, to this day, a school copybook of Cahal Daly's which contains a note to the effect that Cahal had missed two days at school because of the flax-harvesting on a neighbour's farm. In return for his labours, and those of his brothers, his mother was assured of a continuous supply of potatoes and other produce in the winter months of the year.

His childhood memories were of a happy home in the midst of a hard-pressed community. There was hardly a time, he would recall in later years, when he was not aware of problems of great poverty and failures of justice in his own parish and townland. The comparative prosperity of the teacher's household meant that, as a youngster, Cahal would be entrusted by his mother with baskets of home-cooked meals to be delivered to many of their less fortunate neighbours. Clothing too, as soon as he or his brothers and sisters had grown out of it, would be passed on to neighbours' children. This was an accepted practice in those days, households and families exchanging clothing according to need; the Christian community in Loughguile was aware of and attentive to the needs of its members.

This caring was not limited to the Catholics. In Loughguile at least, Christian sensibilities crossed the whole community. There was little, if any, of those antagonisms which were so widespread elsewhere.

Despite earlier folk-memories in the community, such as the time that one McCartney, a bitter Presbyterian, had driven the Catholics out of their church, which happened to be on his land, forcing them to find a new site and build a new church, called "New" to this day, and the church in which the young Cahal Daly was one day to learn to serve Mass, firm and lasting friendships were forged and maintained between Catholics and Protestants, and particularly with those of the Presbyterian faith, who tended to be the owners of some of the larger farm holdings. Thus, the young Cahal Daly grew up in an atmosphere broadly ecumenical and from which friendships have endured to the present day. The Reverend

John Young, Presbyterian minister in Ballymoney, recalls that the young Dalys, John and Cahal, would join him in the cab of his father's horse-drawn bread-van as Mr Young senior would make his morning delivery rounds. Such friendships were an unusual opportunity for young Catholics to understand people of other faiths in Northern Ireland at that time. The seeds of a keen ecumenical spirit were sown in the heart of Cahal Daly from a very early age.

Being the son of the local schoolmaster had certain advantages. One of these was the constant supply of reading matter. His father took the newspaper every day. Part of his task was to pass on the news of the world's events to others in the townland; not everyone had the ability to read and they often depended on the schoolmaster for a knowledge of what was going on in the world outside Loughguile. Young Cahal Daly devoured the daily papers and whatever other printed matter could be found. These were the days before electricity had reached from the cities out into the countryside. All reading, after sundown, had to be done by candlelight. A constant warning to the young Cahal Daly from his grandparents was: don't read so much, you will ruin your eyes! He still remembers the day, while he was yet a child, when the first "Aladdin" paraffin lamp came into the house. He remembers realizing that now, for the first time, he could continue his reading well into the night without the slightest danger to his eyes, or worry to his grandparents!

In accordance with an age-old tradition, not just in Ireland, but throughout the Church in Northern Europe, local clergy would encourage young boys who seemed to be likely candidates for the priesthood, to undertake the study of Latin. Father Rogan, Curate in the "new" church of Loughguile had a keen eye for likely candidates. Young Cahal Daly, together with three other boys from the local school used to go, twice a week, to Father Rogan's house for lessons in Latin and

French. Of the four scholars, only one, Cahal Daly, was eventually to become a priest. It was at Father Rogan's side that there was kindled that love of Latin and French which was to characterize the career of Cahal Daly ever afterwards.

The Catholic atmosphere of both home and school meant that, as he himself was to say many years later, "There never was a time when I did not think of becoming a priest." He remembered being particularly struck by an Augustinian Father who came to preach a retreat in Loughguile during his school days. It was not so much what the priest said that attracted the young schoolboy, as much as the rather splendid habit in which the preacher swept into the church and up into the pulpit.

It was taken as a matter of course that the young Cahal Daly, when the days of primary school were coming to an end, would go to Belfast to sit the scholarship examination for entry into secondary school. If he and his brothers were to have the benefit of a secondary education, then this depended totally on themselves; secondary school fees for his family would have stretched the financial resources of their schoolmaster father beyond limits. The exams were held in far away Belfast. This was a daunting prospect for a youngster of eleven or twelve years. But the journey was made and the exam taken. It was little surprise to anyone who knew him that he passed with flying colours and his course was set for four years at Saint Malachy's College, Belfast.

CHAPTER THREE

Malachy's and Maynooth

Wisdom brings up her own sons,
and cares for those who seek her.
Whoever loves her loves life,
those who wait on her early
will be filled with happiness.
Whoever holds her close
will inherit honour,
and wherever he walks the Lord will bless him.
Those who serve her minister to the Holy One,
and the Lord loves those who love her.

[ECCLESIASTICUS 4:11–16]

SAINT MALACHY'S COLLEGE, BELFAST, was what was known in those days as a Minor Seminary; a secondary school for boys, run by the Catholic Church. It had a dual purpose: to provide general education up to the equivalent of matriculation level for all, and to prepare those of the pupils with an eye on Maynooth with the basics of a clerical education. The Saint Malachy's that the young Cahal Daly entered as a boarder in 1929 was a happy place. Formalities were held at a minimum. There was a school uniform, for instance, of cap, pullover and, for out-of-doors, scarf in the school colours (knitted for each of her sons by Susan Daly). However, after the first week or so of term, uniform was quietly put away and more hardy schoolboy clothing substituted, uniforms being kept for only the more formal occasions. Similarly, the senior boys were supposed to wear gown and mortar-board. Again, these were largely dispensed with, to be worn only when taking examinations.

The atmosphere was open and cheerful. Although classwork and study were taken most seriously (there were four hours of private study-time each day), there was no lack of sports. Cahal Daly soon showed his mettle on the sports field, both in Gaelic football and hurling. Although he never starred, he is remembered as having great speed and determination when "on the ball". In later years, he himself recalled that although he was not a very notable sportsman, he made up in dogged determination what he lacked in skills upon the playing field. There was little opportunity for indulgence in luxuries. Lack of heating meant that each student had to have a rug which was wrapped around the knees during study time. This was no luxury; it was a necessity!

What little pocket-money was available to the students was used to augment the college diet by visits to the local tea-shop. But, more often than not, Cahal Daly preferred to spend his shillings in one or other of the Belfast second-hand bookstores. He became a regular customer in Harry Hall's bookstore in Smithfield, where, as he said, "you could get a load of books for sixpence". His appetite for reading easily enough conquered the appetite for extra food.

The academic year was punctuated by the usual vacations at Christmas, Easter and the long break for the summer holidays. Cahal Daly and his brothers spent these breaks at home in Loughguile, Cahal making sure to bring with him plenty of reading-matter for home consumption.

A vivid memory from those teenage years was that of a family outing, during one holiday from Saint Malachy's, on the occasion of the Eucharistic Congress in 1932. Special pilgrimage trains were put on to carry Catholic pilgrims from Northern Ireland to Dublin and back on the occasion of the great outdoor Mass celebrated in the Phoenix Park. The excitement of the expedition was not diminished by the train having to run the gauntlet of a hail of rocks and other missiles hurled at it from the railside by youngsters of a less than pro-Roman frame of mind!

It was a long day. The Daly family, along with their fellow-pilgrims, detrained at Dublin's Tara Street station and then set out on the long walk westward along the quays of the Liffey to the Phoenix Park where they attended the great High Mass and heard the celebrated voice of Count John McCormack himself as he sang the "Panis Angelicus", the powerful strains echoing across the Fifteen Acres from the loudspeakers erected for the occasion by engineers from the new-born Radio Eireann, whose official opening had been anticipated in order to broadcast the events of the Eucharistic Congress in an historic first-ever link-up with Signore Marconi's Vatican Radio.

After Mass there was the picnic lunch, carefully prepared by Susan Daly the previous day, then the Eucharistic Procession to O'Connell Bridge for Benediction and then the long journey back to Belfast and Loughguile by train.

Stone-throwing committees do not seem to have been on hand to greet the returning pilgrims or their special trains.

The senior students who had matriculated to Queen's University, Belfast, and were known to the other students as "The Queen's Men" remained as boarders in St Malachy's upon the completion of their secondary education, walking to the university for lectures each day. This journey was subject to strict rules. Black, clerical hats were to be worn. No deviation either in route or time taken was allowed; the President of Saint Malachy's announced to the students that he himself had paced the journey and found that it took exactly half an hour. Therefore no more than half an hour was to be allowed for the journey. However, as Cahal Daly and his colleagues, among them the young William Conway, who one day would preceed Cahal Daly in the See of Armagh, soon found out, there were ways and means . . . A small sweetshop, close by the college gates, became an unofficial cloakroom, the young customers regularly leaving their all too easily identified hats there, to be collected again on the way back.

For the students at Saint Malachy's, the study of Latin was obligatory. The importance of the subject was emphasized by the fact that there were two distinct class periods devoted to that language every single day. A chore to some, these periods were a pleasure to young Cahal Daly. He revelled in the study of the classical authors and enjoyed nothing more than to struggle with the translation of an unseen text. His ability was quickly spotted and he found that soon he was being encouraged to undertake the study of the other classical language, Greek. Out of this there grew a new love and Latin and Greek were to become a major element in the preparation of a student who was ever more clearly marked, in the eyes of his tutors, as Maynooth material. The choice of Greek, however, did have one disadvantage; students were allowed to take either Greek or French and thus, because of his choice of Greek, Cahal Daly went through his secondary education without exposure to any modern language, something which he still regrets, but which did not inhibit him from undertaking the study of French at a later stage, with enduring consequences for his ministry, as we shall see.

An honours degree in Classics at Queen's University, Belfast, was perhaps an obvious and certainly enjoyable next step for the young student from Saint Malachy's. It is not surprising, therefore, that the memory of his tutors at that time, remains vivid in Cahal Daly's mind to this day. The encouragement he received from the late James Campbell is gratefully recalled, as were the taxing exercises set by the austere and be-monocled Robert Mitchel Henry, brother of the celebrated Irish landscape painter, Paul Henry. Robert Henry, a Presbyterian, was the author of an authoritative history of the early Sinn Fein. He was anxious to encourage the young classics student to extend his horizons and encouraged him to undertake the study of Milton's Paradise Lost. In later years Cahal Daly was to recall that, "I do not think I ever had my mind stretched as in the Latin classes of Robert Henry." It was Henry who taught the students his own theory of translation which, many years later, Cahal Daly was to recognize as remarkably similar to that of the late Monsignor Ronald Knox in his celebrated work of translating the New Testament. "Translate the meaning; not just the words!" On one occasion Henry had given his charges an apparently obscure piece of prose, to be rendered in the style of Cicero. His insistence was that the students should present him with, not just a translation of words, but with a passage that expressed the meaning of the prose in the original. The students were stymied. "You can't do it," said Henry, eventually, "because it means NOTHING!" The point was made; they could not deliver a meaningful translation because there was precious little meaning in the original. The enjoyment of such academic practical jokes contributed to the enthusiasm which marked the classical studies of Cahal Daly.

In conjunction with his classical studies he undertook and enjoyed an introduction to the world of Scholastic Philosophy under the tutelage of Monsignor Arthur Ryan, one of the outstanding masters of that discipline anywhere in Ireland at the time.

If life in Saint Malachy's was austere, it was no less so further south in the national seminary of Saint Patrick's College, Maynooth. A whole new discipline had to be learned. As was so often the case in such seminaries, conformity was the great criterion. A book of rules, the severity of which would hardly be understood in the later years of the century, was the absolute guiding principle. Silence was the norm; speech was only allowed at certain times and in certain areas. Senior students (those studying Theology) were normally not allowed to mix with the younger philosophers. There was also a long-standing custom, which therefore had the force of law, that students from one diocese (Maynooth catered for the whole of the country) did not normally fraternize with those of another. Each diocese had its own area in the college grounds, where recreation was normally taken. For a student to cross over to the "pos" or position of another diocese to converse with members of that diocese, at least on any regular basis, was taken as a sign of "singularity" and was regarded with severity by the authorities. Persistent singularity would be considered as contra-indicative of a vocation. Persistently "singular" students would eventually be invited to reconsider their calling and to take themselves home, or, as sometimes happened, to colleges of less strict observance where they would often eventually succeed in being ordained, but for dioceses in England, America, or even missions, far from Ireland's shores!

The new student from Saint Malachy's immediately plunged into the study of Theology, and, eager as ever to maximize his opportunities, took, with the agreement of his professors, an extra course, obtaining a Master's degree with a thesis on "The Life of the Church in North Africa in the time of Tertullian", that is to say, the second and third centuries. In preparing for the presentation of his thesis, Cahal Daly spent the summer vacation back in Loughguile, avidly reading in his subject. He found in the writings of Tertullian on the theology of Baptism and Penance an approach which he was fascinated to find weaving its way through the history of theology right up to the writings of the great twentieth-century French theologians such as Henri de Lubac. (And which eventually were to be found coming right through to the theology of the Second Vatican Council, something which was to delight him when, in 1962, he would accompany his bishop, William Philbin of Down and Connor, to Rome as one of his theological advisors at that event.)

Apart from his specialist studies, the standard curriculum of studies at Maynooth left Cahal Daly unsatisfied. The programme of studies was strictly that of the Manuals; a series of theological tracts, by approved authors, which reduced the grandeur and mystery of theological studies, by and large, to the discussion of a series of succinct propositions, supported (very selectively) by quotations from Scripture and from other theologians. Arguments were carefully constructed in order to be demolished by means of quotations similarly selectively used. The young newcomer to theology found this formula approach restricting and stultifying. Fortunately, however, he had as one of his tutors the great William Moran who, sensing his young pupil's dissatisfaction with this pedestrian approach to theology, encouraged him to extend his work and to undertake a study of the notion of ecclesial Collegiality, which he willingly did.

The notion of Collegiality is that doctrine which sees all bishops, by virtue of their episcopal ordination and their communion between themselves and with the Pope as head of the college, as having a corporate responsibility for the whole Church. This concept, which in the normal course of events would have been part of the agenda of the First Vatican Council, where it would have been a necessary counter-balance to the doctrine of Papal Infallibility, was not, in fact, reached at that Council, and had to wait for its formal presentation until the Second Vatican Council. There, as a *peritus*, or expert, Father Daly was to recognize, yet again, a subject which so many years before, he had dedicated himself to during the long winter months in Maynooth.

Besides the set programme of studies, the students were encouraged, in what spare time remained to them, to engage in peripheral activities. This allowed a number of the students to come together and, under the guidance of another of the great names of Maynooth, J. G. McGarry, professor of Sacred Eloquence, (it was not called Preaching or Homiletics in those days) to found the Christus Rex Society. This was a society dedicated to the study and pastoral application of the principles of Sociology. At various times Cahal Daly found himself both Chairmen and Secretary of the young society. Eventually, too, he became editor of the society's journal, *Christus Rex*. Both the society and its magazine were to survive the college years and became a much valued element in the life of many Irish priests; its annual conferences providing the launching platform for many a valuable pastoral initiative. Christus Rex, both as a society and a journal, lasted well into the 1960s by which time it had fulfilled its purpose in preparing the minds of the clergy for the dramatic developments of the Second Vatican Council.

An important indication of the significance of Christus Rex is given by Whyte, in his seminal *Church and State in Modern Ireland*, published by Gill & MacMillan. He says:

> The most important of the new foundations was the Christus Rex Society, which was approved by the Irish bishops in 1945, and held its first conference the following year. Its objects were: "to enlighten public opinion on social questions and to help to form a public conscience sensitive to social abuses and ardent to 'restore all things in Christ'; to promote the study of Catholic social teaching among the clergy and through them among the laity; to inspire coordinated effort by Irish priests for the reform of social evils and the realization in public life of the principles of the Social Encyclicals". Membership was limited to secular priests, but its influence was not confined to them. The papers read at the society's annual conferences have always been well publicized in the press, and since 1947, the society has published the quarterly *Christus Rex*, the principal periodical in Ireland for the discussion of social questions.

Later, in a discussion of opposition in the Church to proposed legal changes with regard to social insurance and legal adoption by the then minister for Social Welfare, William Norton:

> These proposals evoked a barrage of criticism from exponents of Catholic social teaching. The president of *An Riogacht* opposed them. *The Standard* and *Christus Rex* published unfavourable

leading articles. The Catholic Societies Vocational Organization Conference produced an alternative scheme of its own. A particularly violent article was published in *Christus Rex* by a Cork priest, Rev. E. J. Hegarty, which was afterwards published as a pamphlet and used as ammunition by opponents of the scheme. Father Hegarty marked the extreme wing of the opposition, but many of the best-known spokesmen of the Catholic social movement went on record as criticizing the proposals – Fr E. Coyne, SJ, Fr Felim O'Brien, OFM, Dr Cornelius Lucey (then not yet a bishop) and Dr Peter McKevitt. Dr Dignan, Bishop of Clonfert, who, as author of the famous Dignan Plan of 1944 could be considered an authority on such matters, was mildly critical. *Christus Rex* was able to claim, with some justification, that "from those preoccupied with social principle" the proposals had evoked "more criticism than has any contemplated legislation in recent years" . . .

And, on controversies following the famous "Mother and Child scheme" of Dr Noel Browne, *Vigilans*, the commentator of *Christus Rex*, (said):

As the Bishop of Galway said the other day, they [the Irish people] do not seem to understand our language. That was illustrated very clearly during the present year when a great many well-disposed Catholics just could not understand just what was the central objection to the Mother and Child Scheme. We still have a long way to go to make the people as a whole see for themselves the validity of much Catholic social teaching.

Following the Government's modifications to the proposed bill as a result of the Hierarchy's objections:

Some of the exponents of Catholic social teaching also showed dissatisfaction. In July 1953 *Christus Rex* feared that the bill would pass with token amendments, sufficient to avert a condemnation but inadequate to meet the real objections to it. [Subsequently] the changing viewpoint of Catholics with an interest in social questions can be seen by anyone who browses through a run of *Christus Rex*. In the early years, after its foundation in 1947, contributors to this journal seemed more anxious to pass moral judgements than to spend time amassing the facts. By the nineteen-sixties, however, they were far more concerned to provide factual information. The volume for 1964, for instance, contained articles on "employment prospects in the Republic", "merits and problems in planning", "modern research into attitudes towards work" and a survey into young peoples' recreation habits in an Irish town.

Maynooth also afforded the seminarian from Loughguile an opportunity to study the Psalms. The mystery, poetry and, above all, the liturgical use of the Psalms both in the Jewish and the Christian liturgies was, for Cahal Daly, a window into yet another world of delights.

During the subsequent long summer holidays, which were spent *en famille* at Loughguile, the seminarian would not only dedicate himself to furthering his theological studies, but would often undertake to help in his father's school, where he would take the Religious Instruction lessons for the youngsters of the townland. This was a task in which he revelled. Certainly, there was enkindled then a spark of interest in teaching which was to grow, many years later, into the great enjoyment which he got out of his years as a teacher, both in his old college, Saint Malachy's, and in Queen's University, Belfast. It is unlikely that the children in his father's classroom would have realized that they were receiving the benefit of the knowledge and skills of the great catechist, William Moran, as filtered to them through the words of the seminarian son of their schoolmaster:

On those occasions when the regular altar-servers might not have turned up for the daily or Sunday Mass in the parish church, he would stand in and assist the parish priest at the altar.

The end of each academic year at Maynooth was marked by a set of examinations, written and oral, in all the principal theological disciplines. For Cahal Daly and his classmates the most serious of these, of course, were those taken in the spring of 1941, prior to priestly ordination. It was not unknown for students who did not do well in these exams to have their ordinations postponed. The atmosphere, in those final months, therefore, was somewhat tense. On the morning of the final examination in Dogmatic Theology, however, Cahal Daly was feeling confident. He felt he knew that he could deliver what his professor, Dr Moran, would require. The candidates sat down. The papers were distributed, face down, and at a signal, all turned over their papers and began to read. All around him, students began to write. There was no time to be lost; there was a lot of ground to be covered in two hours. Cahal Daly's pen remained untouched. He read the examination paper from beginning to end. Then he read it again. He knew his professor. He knew the way his mind worked. He also knew that something special was expected from himself. For a full hour and fifteen minutes the answer paper in front of him remained blank. He could sense the eyes of his fellow students on him. He knew what they were thinking. Aha! Daly is stuck this time. Moran has him! But they were wrong. After an hour and a quarter's intense thought, Cahal Daly picked up his pen and began to write. His paper was finished on the stroke of time.

The result: First in his class. Neither he nor his professor had expected anything else. The way was now open to Ordination.

In the spring months of 1941, throughout the length and breadth of Ireland, parents and families were preparing for Ordination Day. It had been customary for the immediate

families of the Ordinands to come to Maynooth where the
ordinations took place in the huge Gothic college chapel. They
would normally stay in local hotels and guests houses in order
to return to the college on the next morning for the new priests'
First Masses. In 1941, however, things were to be different.
This was wartime. And although the Irish Free State was
neutral, nevertheless, the Irish economy was so inextricably
bound to that of Britain that Ireland too was suffering from
rationing. There was little petrol to be had and thus few cars
on the roads. The Daly family, however, like many others,
had made special plans. Petrol had been somehow acquired
and saved up for the journey from Loughguile. And, there
being no family car, arrangements had been made to borrow
the car of a neighbour.

But the war had had another effect; Maynooth was bursting
at the seams. The war in Europe and, before that, the Spanish
Civil War, had meant that students in the Irish Colleges in
Salamanca and Paris had been all brought back to Ireland to
finish their studies and to be ordained.

Faced with this unprecedented accommodation problem and,
it was claimed, in order not to embarrass those students whose
families could not arrange to come to Maynooth for the
ordinations, the college authorities, a few short weeks before
the event, decreed that no families would be invited to the
ordinations at all! However, in order to ease the
disappointment, it was also arranged that, instead of remaining
in the college to celebrate their First Masses, the new priests
would be free to return to their families and homes immediately
after their ordinations and to celebrate their First Masses in
their parish churches. This meant that, in fact, the Daly family,
as did so many others, did, in fact, travel to Maynooth by car
that weekend, many arriving a day early in the vain hope that
the college authorities might have a change of heart and that
they might, after all, witness their sons' ordinations. But it was

not to be. The parish church of Maynooth village was unusually full for Mass that day, whilst a few hundred yards away, on the other side of the college wall, their sons were being anointed with the oil of salvation at the hands of Dublin's newly appointed young archbishop; the Most Reverend John Charles McQuaid, in the first ordinations of his episcopate.

Immediately following the ceremony, Father Cahal Daly and his family set off on the long drive to Belfast and Loughguile. And the war was to have yet another effect on that day as the Dalys, in their borrowed car, left the city of Belfast and headed further north for home, the air-raid sirens sounded out and Adolf Hitler launched a bombing raid on Belfast. But by the time the first bombs fell, the car was well on its way and next day, June 23rd 1941, Father Cahal Daly celebrated his First Mass at the altar of the parish church of Loughguile.

To James

Pray, brethren, that my Sacrifice and yours
may be acceptable to God the Father Almighty.

In Grateful Remembrance

OF

My Ordination

IN

The College Chapel, Maynooth

AND OF

My First Holy Mass

IN

Loughguile

June 22nd and 23rd, 1941

✠

CAHAL DALY

✠

The Spirit of the Lord is upon me : where-
fore He hath anointed me to preach the Gospel
to the poor. He hath sent me to heal the
contrite of heart "—*Luke* iv. 18.

Mother of Divine Grace, Refuge of Sinners,
pray for me.

CHAPTER FOUR

Paris in the Springtime

A much travelled man knows many things,
and a man of great experience will talk sound sense.
Someone who has never had his trials knows little,
but the travelled man is master of every situation.

[ECCLESIASTICUS 34:9–11]

THE YEAR 1946 saw an appointment to the teaching staff of Queen's University, Belfast, as Lecturer in Scholastic Philosophy. Despite a self-confessed lack of training in the art of teaching Philosophy (it had been no more than a subsidiary subject in his studies up to now), Father Daly found his new appointment a challenge, and an enjoyable one. He admitted, at times, to having to struggle to keep a page or two ahead of his students in the current text books. Nevertheless, he subsequently described these teaching days as a "voyage of discovery". He felt that he had, in a sense, "grown away" from Classics and so it was with a certain feeling of homecoming that he now rediscovered his Greek studies.

Queen's University had, in the time of Cardinal Mac Rory, been described by that prelate as "having a non-Catholic atmosphere". It was, after all, one of the educational bastions of the then British Empire. Nevertheless, over the years, things had improved for Catholics. It was to Queen's that the young students from Saint Malachy's College went to be introduced to the Groves of Academe. It was from the study of Philosophy at Queen's that the young seminarians went on to the study of Theology at Maynooth.

For reasons that were both historical and not too difficult

to understand, Queen's had in fact two departments of Philosophy; General Philosophy and Scholastic Philosophy. In practical terms this ensured that young Catholic students of Philosophy (almost all of them candidates for the priesthood) would attend the lectures in Scholastic Philosophy, based as they were on the teachings of the great Dominican philosopher and theologian, Saint Thomas Aquinas, whilst Protestant students were catered for in the other department. Further, it was strictly forbidden for a Catholic to enrol in or attend lectures in the "other" department. It was in the "Catholic" department that Cahal Daly's duties lay.

However, in the months and years following his appointment to that department, Father Daly found little or no trace of anti-Catholicism among either students or faculty. The diminutive cleric became a familiar figure about the campus, although, because of the "secular" nature of the institution, he was excused from the obligation to wear clerical dress, and would have normally worn the ordinary collar and tie under a dark suit and academic gown. He was also easily recognized in the environs of the university, not just by reason of the shiny black Volkswagen "Beetle" that he drove, but also for the abandon with which he drove it. It was said (albeit affectionately) by both faculty and students, that he was by far the worst driver in the history of motoring! This reputation was enhanced when, in the fullness of time, the original VW was pensioned off and the young priest equipped himself with a new model having the advantage of a 1300 cc engine: the most powerful thing then available in Volkswagens. This was reputed to have caused general consternation on the campus.

On one occasion, when having a cup of morning coffee in the local coffee bar, known as the "Queen's Espresso", where he often went and where he had a favourite table, at which he would sit alone and undisturbed, he fell into conversation with a group of businessmen at the next table. They were what might be called hard-headed Sandy Row Protestants, and they had no idea of the identity of the young academic with whom they were talking. After he had gone back to his duties, one of the group was heard to say: "Quite a nice fellow. But from something he said, I think he may be a Catholic." There was, however, a dumbfounded silence when another member of the University staff, on passing their table, leaned over to them and said: "Yes, he is a Catholic, and not only that, but he is a priest too." Perhaps, unbeknown to himself, Father Daly had done a little bit to counteract that underpinning of prejudice on which so much of Belfast society was based.

Nevertheless, in later years, Cahal Daly remembered only the warmth with which he was received by his colleagues and his students alike.

In this agreeable academic atmosphere he threw himself into the study of the renewal of Scholastic Philosophy and found himself fascinated by the writings of a certain Father Sertillanges in this field. His study in Sertillanges served to prepare his mind and his appetite for the next stage in his academic career, for it was while he was on the teaching faculty at Queen's that an opportunity occurred which was to change his perception of his priesthood, his ministry, and of the Church itself: he was offered the chance of taking a Sabbatical. The choice was of staying in Ireland, or going to Rome, Louvain or Paris. In a choice which was to prove providential, he opted for Paris. His reason was simple: there were, at the time, no Irish priests studying in Paris and none of the clergy currently teaching Philosophy in Ireland had been trained there. And there he would have an opportunity to study the French Church and French history and culture. There might even be something to bring back to flesh-out and balance the strongly Rome-orientated attitudes of the Church and church educational institutions at home.

He had already made brief visits to Lourdes and Lisieux in

the summer of 1950. He had found himself fascinated by the French Church. The pastoral letters of Cardinal Souhard, then Archbishop of Paris, on the problems of the Church in France and his visions of its future were compelling reading. The Cardinal's pastoral insights captivated him then and those same pastoral letters continued to be regular reading matter for Cahal Daly right up to the time when he himself had to accept the burdens of episcopacy.

The summer of 1951 was spent tramping through the streets and alleys of Paris on a seemingly endless search for student quarters in which he could establish himself for the coming academic year. Convents, colleges, hostels, digs, all were full. The whole of the francophone student world, from Canada to West Africa and the Far East, seemed to be heading for Paris that autumn, and all had got their bookings in before Cahal Daly. Eventually, however, in a leafy suburb, not far from the Latin Quarter, he found the small hostel run by the *Benedictines Missionaires*, who were happy to accept the young Irish priest under their roof. The setting was quiet and comfortable, and it was but a short metro ride to the Institut Catholique, the College de France, the Sorbonne, the Luxembourg Gardens, the "Boule Miche" and the whole complex that was the student Paris of the Fifties and Sixties.

There too were the small cafés and bookstores which were to become such an important part of his life.

The whole of France, and Paris in particular, was still recovering from the devastation of World War II. Rebuilding of cities, towns and villages was still under way. The euphoria of *la Libération* was still in the air. A barber, who cut the young Irish priest's hair shortly after his arrival, spoke excitedly of having been present in the Cathedral of Notre Dame for the singing of the Te Deum to celebrate the *Libération*; "That is what heaven will be like," he said, "the chanting of the Te Deum on Liberation Day." And for the rest of his own life, the sound of the Te Deum has always reminded Cahal Daly of those days in post-war Paris.

The city was aglow that autumn, and the young Father Daly revelled in it. His main studies, in Metaphysics, Moral Philosophy and Theology were carried out at the Institut Catholique. But the other institutes of learning were open to him also. Quiet personal study could as well be done in the shady setting of the Luxembourg Gardens, or at a table in one of the many cafés. There, for the price of a single *café noir* or *café crême*, the student priest could sit and read or write for an entire morning or afternoon. Nobody bothered him. There were no questions. Occasional hunger pangs were often assuaged by chunks of Cadbury's Whole-Nut milk chocolate which were regularly mailed out to him from Belfast by his sister, Sheila. Among the other students, and the academics too, the same cafés and bistros were the setting for many a long and even taxing philosophical discussion, held, with vigour, over the course of a simple meal. There was something eminently satisfactory to find Philosophy or Theology being done in such civilized surroundings. Here the word "intellectual" had none of the pejorative overtones that it so often seemed to have in the islands further to the north. If you were an intellectual, you were an intellectual and the intellectuals were recognized as having something of value to offer both society and the Church.

One aspect of Parisian academic life worried Cahal Daly; the formality of the University lectures and the distance at which the professors and tutors held themselves from the student body.

This, as he was to learn, was a natural defence mechanism. The faculty members were saving their energies and their precious time for research. They were reluctant to enter into any kind of dialogue with their students. Certainly not in the academic hall. One simply did not interrupt the *Maître* during the course of a lecture. Nor could you buttonhole any of them after lectures. They had perfected the technique of the quick getaway. Their telephones were always ex-directory. The lesson of all this was that you got your material first time off and subsidiary questions were dealt with by research in private study. All this, however, did not totally inhibit the young *prêtre* from Ireland. He was known to ask the occasional question in class, and he did manage to make personal contact with those professors with whom he felt he needed contact. It was totally alien to him to be merely a passive recipient of their wisdom. He needed something more. And occasionally he got it. Even the great Gabriel Marcel was not spared the occasional knock on his apartment door by the young Irishman hungry for further knowledge.

These were unhappy days for the Church in France. It had been said that at any one time, fifty per cent of the French clergy were in Rome, denouncing the preaching and teaching of the other fifty per cent. Although this was said in jest, as is often the case, there was more than a crumb of truth behind the joke. Denunciations there certainly were. And, unfortunately, some people in the Roman Curia were innocent enough (or worse, vindictive enough) to take notice. The result was a period of great unhappiness in the Church in France. The tragic and scandalous upshot of it all was the silencing of some of the most celebrated Catholic teachers of that time, among them Fathers Chenu, Yves Congar, the Dominican, and the Jesuit, Henri de Lubac. The agony of these men was shared by their loyal students, among them Cahal Daly. They suffered with their masters, often puzzling in their minds how such injustices could have been allowed to happen. The work of Father Congar on the Christian Fathers was particularly important to Cahal Daly who found a particular fascination in being able to trace the roots of modern Ecclesiology in the work of the Fathers. To find his mentor falling under Vatican disapproval was a painful experience. However, the attitudes of the victimized professors, with their courage and patience, were recognized by their students as, in some enigmatic and mysterious way, the work of the Holy Spirit. Just how these tribulations would contribute to the splendour of the Church would only become apparent a quarter of a century later.

Among those who were painfully aware of all that was going on was the rotund and affable Apostolic Nuncio to France, one Angelo Giuseppe Roncalli. The new, secular France was scarcely inclined to take either the Vatican or its representative seriously. He became noted in Paris for his *gaffes*, particularly in his struggles with the French language. Once as professor at Rome's Lateran Seminary, he had been removed from office there for teaching "unsafe" doctrines to his young seminarists, so he knew what it was for an academic to suffer. Undoubtedly his opinions on the problems of the theologians were sought in Rome, but his word was as nothing compared to those strong forces of the extreme Right who were firmly ensconced about the Papal throne. Roncalli, however, was a man of calm disposition and patience. Although there is no accessible record, it is more than likely that he could have had a private, encouraging word with the suffering academics. Certainly, in the long run, he was instrumental in vindicating the injured in a most dramatic way . . . But this is to jump ahead.

Meantime, one of the most impressive acts, by the gravely wronged Father de Lubac, was his writing, in the Jesuit intellectual revue, *Etudes*, an article entitled "The Church, Our Mother". This was a generous act of humility on the part of the young Jesuit. There was no sign of rancour. The article was a quiet, theologically impeccable study of the caring Church, and was one with which even his enemies could not find fault. The article would subsequently appear as one of the chapters in his celebrated book, *The Splendour of the Church*, to be published when the dark clouds of suspicion and recrimination had eventually been dispelled. But meanwhile, one of the most outstanding aspects of the whole era was the palpable spirit of calm patience exhibited by the victims. It was an example never to be forgotten by their students.

All of this was witnessed by Cahal Daly and his fellow students at the Institut Catholique with great pain and bewilderment. Their sadness, shared by a whole generation of Catholics, equally puzzled and distressed by what was going on, was soothed by the great nobility and obedience of the victims. They gave an example of that patience which in grace is the reward of the unjustly victimized.

With the wisdom of hindsight, of course, it is somewhat easier to see what was happening. Justice did eventually triumph. The disgraced theologians were reinstated most dramatically when, in the fullness of time, the erstwhile Nuncio in France, after a spell as Patriarch of Venice now become Pope John XXIII, announced his great Ecumenical Council, Vatican II, and the names of the once disgraced theologians were to become celebrated throughout the Catholic world as the great theological names of that Council. At the Council, too, one Father Cahal Daly, by now himself one of the *periti* or theological experts of the Council, would be able to renew his acquaintance with his old masters, and indeed, on occasions found himself shoulder-to-shoulder with his old friend and mentor, Father de Lubac, in the special tribune reserved for the theologians at the Council sessions in Saint Peter's.

When asked, in a BBC interview in 1990, what he thought those unhappy days in Paris had contributed to the life and history of the Church, Cahal Daly, by then a bishop, answered unhesitatingly: Those days contributed the Second Vatican Council!

However, Paris in the Fifties was not all doom and gloom. Academic life had to go on, and there was plenty to stimulate a young mind. There were the days of the flourishing of Existentialism. If the black soutanes of the clergy were to be seen in the colleges and the cafés of the student quarter, they were not the only ones in black. The black shirts of those who would have thought themselves followers of Jean-Paul Sartre and others of the new enlightenment were there too. One such was a young Irish artist and sculptor, then studying in the *atelier* of the noted French artist, Fernand Leger, Ray Carroll. Leger, who with Picasso and Matisse, was of the front line amongst the artistic establishment in post-war France was, despite his appearance (he always dressed in dark suit, with shirt and necktie, having the appearance of nothing other than a minor French civil servant) the perfect Man of the Left. His students, including Carroll, often remarked how little sense of humour he displayed. He did, however, sow one important seed in the mind of his young Irish student: Art must always be at the service of The People, a sentiment which, of course, underlies all liturgical art — not that that would have been a consideration with Leger himself, or Ray Carroll at that time!

Ray Carroll, in later years, would have thought of how often he would have passed the young Father Daly on the "Boule Miche" and looked with fashionable scorn on his clerical habit. Both priest and artist were forming themselves, imbibing the heady atmosphere of post-liberation Paris. Both were to meet again, one day, in their native Ireland in circumstances which at that time they could never have envisaged.

The doctrines of Sartre and his disciples were a challenge for Cahal Daly and his colleagues. Daly himself was engaged in the study of the philosophy of Saint Thomas Aquinas. His study, however, was not of a dead philosophical system, but rather of Neo-Thomism, which sought to apply the principles of the great Doctor's theories to an understanding of the modern world, an exercise which in itself he found a fascinating pursuit.

Those were days in which even the ordinary daily newspapers would be caught up in great intellectual debates between the schools and institutes. Quality papers, such as *Le Monde* and *Le Figaro* would dedicate columns and, indeed pages, to these philosophical debates. They were read avidly by the student body. Cahal Daly remembered them as "duels fought with words". Among the most memorable was a protracted debate, carried on in the pages of *Les Temps Modernes* in which Jean-Paul Sartre and Albert Camus debated the political applications of the principles of philosophy. The whole debate was carried out with controlled rhetoric and passion. Cahal Daly and his friends revelled in these intellectual fireworks and devoured the material as it was published, day by day, segment by segment, debate after debate.

However stimulating or intellectually exciting, Paris is not France, nor France, Paris. Very quickly the young Belfast priest became fascinated by the church art and architecture of that country which had been dubbed the "Oldest Daughter of the Church". As a result, he took whatever opportunity might arise to move out of Paris and to revel in the architectural glories of France. His explorations took him the length and breadth of the land. He was forcibly struck with the underdevelopment of rural France. Agricultural technology was little different from what he would have seen in the fields of Antrim twenty years earlier. Peasant life was slowly and laboriously emerging from the travails of war.

It was his ambition, eventually realized, to visit every one of the French *régions* and to experience their great churches and cathedrals. There he sat and sometimes prayed, at other times simply marvelled at those pinnacles of human achievement, whether the soaring *flèches* of Rheims and Rouen, at one extreme, or the stark simplicity of the Matisse chapel at Vence on the other. Many years afterwards, he would look back to those journeys of discovery and speak of the sense of wonder that the great medieval cathedrals evoked. "Nowadays we marvel at the wonders of technology that allow us to send men to the moon and back," he would say, "but the men who built those cathedrals had no computers. They were working out the architectural principles as they went along. They were exploring science for the glory of God, and look what monuments to their own faith they produced!"

At that time his deep interest in the ecclesiastical art and architecture was simply a necessary part of his study of French history and culture. He had no inkling, at that time, that the experience gained would one day be put to practical use back in Ireland when he would be a member of the Irish Bishops' Liturgical Commission, and would, indeed, end by invoking some of those same principles in the building of churches himself.

Back in Paris, at weekends Sunday would be celebrated by attending Mass in one or other of those churches noted for their liturgies. Those were the days when Paris was leading the world in the development of pastoral liturgy. Through the worship experience at Saint Sulpice and other similar venues, he learned that the art of Liturgy, far from being a mere matter of rubrics, as had been the case back in Maynooth, was here a means to the development of a liturgical community and was, moreover, a striking means of spiritual catechesis.

Whenever time could be afforded away from the severe regime of study that he set himself, Cahal Daly loved to wander through the Louvre, the Orangerie or one or other of the great galleries. "I was intoxicated by the splendours of the Louvre," he said. Occasionally he would allow himself the luxury of a journey up Montmartre to the Place du Tertre where he would stroll amongst the artists as they stood at their easels under the plane trees capturing the brilliant white of the dome of the Sacré Coeur against the blue of the sky, or the swirling colours of the passing traffic by the Moulin Rouge. It was invigorating for him to find himself in a society which took art and ideas seriously. Life was a celebration: a celebration of creativity.

Ireland had a contribution to make too. It was a proud evening for him when the noted Irish academic, Seamus O Delargy, founder of the Irish Folklore Institute, and a fellow Antrim man, came to speak at the Sorbonne. His paper was about his life's work in and for the Institute, and his words were greeted with enthusiastic plaudits by the assembled academics. The lecture and the reception which followed were a milestone in the course of Cahal Daly's academic year.

Most notable of all, perhaps, was that day when, studies completed, he was awarded his Master's degree, the *Licentiatus* in Philosophy at the Institut Catholique. His next task was to bring back to Ireland, not only his academic honours, but that incalculable wealth of experience from which not only he, but all who were subsequently to work with him, would undoubtedly benefit.

CHAPTER FIVE

The *Peritus*

If you wish, my son,
you can acquire instruction,
if you give your mind to it, subtlety will be yours.
If you love listening you will learn,
if you lend an ear, wisdom will be yours.
Attend the gathering of elders;
if there is a wise man there, attach yourself to him.

[ECCLESIASTICUS 6:32–5]

THE SECOND VATICAN COUNCIL of the Roman Catholic Church was the twenty-first ecumenical council in the history of the Church and it was The Council that Went Wrong. It "went wrong" under the guidance of the Holy Spirit. When the bishops of the world gathered in the basilica of Saint Peter, Rome, on October 9th, 1962, they were in receipt of a series of documents which they did not like and which they proceeded to reject.

The preparation for the Council had begun shortly after the startling announcement by Pope John XXIII, on January 25th, 1959, that he intended to call an Ecumenical Council. There had not been such for almost a century, the First Vatican Council having broken up in disarray at the outbreak of the Franco-Prussian War in 1870.

Pope John had had three purposes in calling "his" council; A spiritual and evangelical renewal of the Church, an updating of the work and methods of the Catholic Church (the so-called "*aggiornamento*"), and the furtherance of the work of Christian unity.

All the bishops of the Catholic world were invited to send in their suggestions as to what should form the agenda for the Council. Over 9,000 proposals were received. The coordination of all this material was entrusted to a series of ten preparatory commissions who worked on it from November 1960 to June 1962. The result was a series of twenty texts which were then handed on to a Central Preparatory Commission, who revised the documents before submitting them for Pope John's approval. Then, a selection of these were sent out to the bishops as the agenda for the first session of the Council.

As soon as they arrived at Rome, it became clear to the bishops that the revised documents, as issued to them, did not, in fact, represent either their consensus or the suggestions which they had submitted, but rather the theology and attitudes of the preparatory commissions, who had edited and filtered their material in such a way that the Council was in danger of failing to achieve the ends set out for it by the Pope. As they saw it, the Church was in danger of becoming lodged in the nineteenth century instead of confronting the twentieth, as had been the intention of John XXIII. So, the documents were rejected and the work began again with new Commissions elected by the bishops themselves and with the approval of the Holy Father. The Council had "gone wrong" and many saw this decisive corrective action by the Pope and the episcopal participants as a sign that the Holy Spirit was indeed with them and that she (the Hagia Sophia of old) would guide them in their deliberations from that day on.

The bishops did not travel to the Council alone. They brought with them their *periti*, or expert advisors. This was necessary because, although the work of a Council is essentially theological, not all bishops were in any way expert theologians. In fact, in the Church of the 1950s the majority of bishops would have been appointed as a result of their qualifications in Canon Law rather than in theology.

The Bishop of Down and Connor, Bishop William Philbin, brought with him, as his *peritus*, Father Cahal Daly.

Life for the *periti* at the First Session of the Council could have been very dull, for, although, as theological advisors to the bishops, they had been brought by their bishops to Rome, they were not allowed into Saint Peter's for the business sessions of the Council. The Vatican, as has so often been the case, both before and since, was obsessed by secrecy. Oaths of secrecy were exacted at every hand's turn. So the theologians, whose only reason for being in Rome was to advise their bishops in the course of the Council, were not allowed into the Council! They had to depend for their information on second-hand sources.

Not only were they themselves dismayed and exasperated by such attitudes, but many of their bishops were too. As a result, the interpretation of the rule of secrecy differed markedly from one bishop to another and from the bishops of one country or continent to another.

The Vatican had set up an office for the dissemination of what material it deemed suitable for release. But the documents which came out from this official *Sala Stampa* were so filtered and so bland that both the world's press and those others who were in Rome on the official business of the bishops decided that an alternative source was imperative. As a result, the Dutch Church on one hand and the Bishops of the United States of America on the other, set up briefing agencies of their own. Week after week, the Americans held press conferences in the basement of the USO, their general rendezvous point at the other end of the Via Conciliazione from Saint Peter's, and the Dutch established IDOC, an information agency which operated from an office in that huddle of buildings which house the headquarters of the Jesuit Fathers on the Via Penitenzieri, in the very shadow of Saint Peter's itself.

It was to these agencies that the deprived *periti*, including Father Cahal Daly, had to have recourse to find out what exactly was going on inside the Aula of the Council itself, although, to be fair, Bishop William Conway, present at first as Auxiliary to Cardinal Dalton of Armagh, and later to be present at subsequent sessions in his own right as Archbishop of Armagh and later Cardinal, did "feed" the unfortunate *periti* whatever information he felt entitled to impart without violating the secrecy of the Council as he saw it.

There were many stories of the borrowing or otherwise purloining of monsignorial robes by frustrated *periti* intent on stealing a few precious hours inside the sessions of the Council itself. Thus it was that, on a few occasions, a totally spurious "Monsignor Daly" did in fact gain some immediate personal experience of the working of the Council at that stage. He also, on one memorable occasion, was spotted by an eagle-eyed attendant. On that occasion he was not "in disguise", but wearing on his plain priest's cassock a poor imitation of the official identity-pass. On this occasion he was unceremoniously hustled from the basilica in a manner more congruent with a James Cagney movie than with the august surroundings of the Vatican. Just something to be chalked up to experience (what else, for a Philosopher?) and savoured later in the coffee-bars as other similarly straitened *periti* recounted comparable adventures.

In the long run, however, as a result of the protestations of the bishops themselves, particularly the Americans, the Canadians and the French, the rules governing the attendance of *periti* at subsequent sessions of the Council were considerably relaxed, and the theologians were, of course, able to be of much more assistance to their bishops. It has to be said, however, that, despite its protestations to the contrary, the Vatican in its communications machinery, to this day has remained relatively paranoid with regard to its dealing with the outside world, and particularly with the international press.

Father Cahal Daly lived, during the Council, at the Irish College, on the other side of the city from the Vatican, close by the basilica of Saint John Lateran. He and his colleagues, the *periti* of the other bishops, spent the many enforced hours of waiting in exploring the glories of Rome and its environs. Those were golden, autumn days of sunshine and cool breezes and many were the expeditions to the surrounding hillside towns of Frascati, Castel Gandolfo, Orvieto . . . For Cahal Daly it was a welcome opportunity to renew acquaintance with those names and places so familiar to him from the days of his classical studies.

Back at the Irish College in the evenings, however, there was often work to be done. Bishop Conway did succeed in conveying to his younger priest-helper something of the excitement of the conciliar debates. The French and German bishops had smelt blood in their examination of the preparatory documents and had set out to spike the guns of those who would have emasculated the Council from the beginning. He himself rejoiced to witness the cut and thrust of the ensuing debates. "I have seen the pages of history being turned," he said.

Outside the walls of the Vatican, at the Domus Pacis, a religious house on the Aurelian Way, a series of lectures was arranged by some of the Council Fathers and their more senior *periti*. Cahal Daly and his colleagues eagerly attended these sessions and heard the conciliar wisdom from the lips of such luminaries as Fathers de Lubac, Congar, Ratzinger, Küng and Colombo, all of whose names, in one way or another, were to adorn the pages of Church history for the quarter of a century to come. For Cahal Daly, there was the added pleasure of seeing and hearing, once more, those men whose work and patience he had so admired all those years ago in Paris. Among them, Fathers Congar and de Lubac, for so long silenced, were now reaping the reward of their heroic patience. The Fathers of the Council as well as so many others of the faithful, worldwide, who were thirsting for that news of progress in the

Council which the official Vatican "Information Services" were denying them, were now benefiting from the collective theological and spiritual wisdom of those great minds at their regular, extracurricular evening sessions.

Two of the early conciliar documents which have since become recognized as cardinal points in the whole output of Vatican II were those concerned with the nature of the Church itself, entitled "*Lumen Gentium*" ("The Light of the World") and with the work of the Church in the modern world, entitled "Gaudium et Spes", from its opening words in Latin, "Joy and Hope". The Irish episcopal delegates were to play an important part in the preliminary drafting of these documents, and with them, of course, their theological advisors. In later years, Bishop Daly was, in all natural modesty, to deny that any of his own words were to be recognized in the eventual Council documents. Nevertheless, it was well known that Bishop, later Cardinal, Conway had a deep regard for the substantial contributions of his *peritus* during those working sessions at the Irish College and one would not have had to be an ex-pupil of the great R. M. Henry oneself to recognize the style of his one-time pupil in sections of the graceful Latin texts as they eventually appeared. Once again, during the preparatory committee-work on these texts, notably on "*Gaudium et Spes*" the young Irish *peritus* had the pleasure of working alongside his great heroes of the Paris days, Fathers Congar, de Lubac and Colombo. On one occasion, as he was sitting with Père de Lubac, this time as a totally recognized and officially admitted *peritus*, in the special tribune in Saint Peter's reserved for them, he remembers listening to a young Bishop Karol Wojtyla, from Poland, make a particularly telling intervention. The elderly Frenchman turned to his young Irish companion and said: "What a wonderful Pope that man would make!" The rest is history.

As the theologian Joseph Komonchak has said: Vatican II represents a turning-point in the Catholic Church, a moment in her self-realization that has only begun to reveal its truth and power. Cahal Daly could consider it no other than a tremendous grace from God to have been able to make such a personal contribution to so momentous an event.

CHAPTER SIX

The Bishop:
Ardagh and Clonmacnoise

Like clay in the hands of the potter
to mould as it pleases him,
so are men in the hands of their Maker
to reward as he judges right.

[ECCLESIASTICUS 33:13]

ON FRIDAY, MAY 26th, 1967, Father Cahal Daly was summoned from his mother's home on Rosetta Avenue, Belfast, to the Apostolic Nunciature in Dublin's Phoenix Park. There the Nuncio, Archbishop Censi, told him that it was the will of the Holy Father, Pope Paul VI, that he should become Bishop of the diocese of Ardagh and Clonmacnoise.

Cahal Daly was genuinely shattered. True, there had been the usual clerical rumours that he might be offered the position, but those rumours did not penetrate, in any strength at least, to his academic seclusion at Queen's, where, in addition to his university duties, he was busily engaged in researching and writing a history of the Maynooth Christus Rex Society. Any hint of the appointment that might have reached him he would have dismissed as idle and highly unlikely speculation. On one occasion when his duties as an external examiner to Maynooth entailed a lunch with his colleagues in the old Alma Mater, one of them, Father John Corkery, erstwhile Librarian at Maynooth and then ministering in the diocese of Ardagh and Clonmacnoise, teasingly said, "Cahal, I know the members of the Longford town Brass Band. What music would you like played when you come to Longford as Bishop?" The suggestion was greeted with horror by Daly: "John, you know perfectly well that those rumours are not true!"

Now, however the axe had fallen. Here he was, a dyed-in-the-wool academic being asked to accept an office and a burden for which he genuinely felt himself unequipped. He had never even been a curate, let alone a parish priest! What could he possibly know of pastoral matters? Yet, Rome had spoken, and he felt himself in no position to decline. And so, he accepted.

As he left the ornate Victorian villa that was the Nunciature and drove through the spring sunshine in the Phoenix Park towards Dublin and the road back north it would have been a matter of speculation as to who was in the greater state of shock, the fallow deer who started at the sound of the little black Volkswagen Beetle or the diminutive cleric behind its wheel.

There followed a terrible week. As is normal in these circumstances, the Papal Nuncio had put him under what is called "The Pontifical Secret"; he could tell nobody, not even his mother, with whom he lived, nor any of his closest friends or colleagues. The secret was to be most strictly guarded until twelve o'clock, noon, on the following Friday, June 2nd, Feast of the Sacred Heart of Jesus, when there was to be a press conference to announce the appointment. Only one other person was there with whom he could talk, Cardinal William Conway of Armagh who, of course, would have had an important part in helping the Pope to make his selection. The two spoke by telephone, and Cardinal Conway suggested that he himself would like to be the one to break the news to Susan Daly that her son was to be the new bishop. He arranged that, one hour before the official announcement, he would telephone Mrs Daly and congratulate her. Her son diplomatically arranged that he would be gone from the house by that time, but told his mother before he left for Mass with the Good

Shepherd Sisters nearby, that there might be a call from the cardinal at about eleven o'clock, and would she be ready to take the message. Alas for the best laid plans. The nation's press had, of course, been issued with a press-release, under strict embargo until noon. But the strain was too much for one eager reporter and so, at half past ten, thirty minutes before the scheduled call from the cardinal, Mrs Daly got a telephone call from one of the papers. They simply asked her one question: How does it feel to be the mother of a bishop? Her son returned from his Mass to find her just as shocked as he had been a week before, despite the comforting and reassuring words of Cardinal Conway who had, as arranged, called her at eleven o'clock, only to find that his thunder had been stolen. And the bishop-elect had learned his first lesson in dealing with the press.

On July 14th, 1967, Cahal Daly motored from Belfast to Longford town and presented his letters of appointment to the Dean and Chapter of Saint Mel's cathedral. Two days later, on the feast of Our Lady of Mount Carmel, a bright, sunny day, he was ordained bishop by the Papal Nuncio with the cardinal and Bishop Farren of Derry as the two co-consecrators. The ceremony took place beneath the towering pinnacles of the Gothic high altar, a strange intrusion into the classical Hiberno-Romanesque sanctuary of Saint Mel's. It was an altar that, before long, was to play an unexpectedly large part in the ministry of the new bishop.

The episcopal ring that was placed on his finger and the pastoral staff which was placed in his hand on that day had been blessed the night before by Cardinal Conway who had come down from Armagh and stayed the night.

The diocese of Ardagh and Clonmacnoise, after a whole year *sede vacante* since the death of the previous bishop, the stately James Joseph MacNamee, who had ruled the diocese for all of forty years, once more had a bishop. A bishop, indeed, whose first and formidable task was to get to know the priests and people of the diocese. He knew no-one there! Often afterwards, the new bishop was to remark that the warmth of the welcome given to him by both clergy and people was the one thing that remained firm in his memory of a year, the first months of which were otherwise a whirl of activity, of which no other clear memory remains. His spare time was spent in studying both the history and the geography of his diocese. Rapidly he devised a "job spec" for himself. His priorities were to be: To be available for personal contact with both priests and people, on an informal basis.

Barriers and distances of misplaced awe were to be eliminated and replaced by one-to-one contact.

"It matters", he said, "that the material living conditions of the priests are attended to; that clerical sickness benefit and retirement arrangements are adequate. It matters to people that letters be answered and their business attended to; it matters to the needy that adequate welfare funds and schemes are built up; it matters to priests and people that careful planning be devoted to the building, renovation and maintenance of schools and churches.

"I must be a teacher of Christian faith and living to all. I must be able to give doctrinal and moral guidance on the many problems confronting Christians today, at personal, family, social and political levels. I must be in touch with theological development in the Church as a whole, and with intellectual trends of the surrounding culture.

"I must at all costs find time for personal prayer, since I must be, above all else, a sanctifier of priests, religious and people, a leader in prayer and an animator of the life of the Spirit."

This was an agenda to which his every endeavour has been to adhere and which, in retrospect, provides a clue to the motivation behind many of those things which were to be milestones in his episcopate and which, from time to time, were the object of criticism by those less informed in the theology of Episcopacy.

The importance of the sacred Liturgy in the life of the Church had been one of the first subjects addressed by the Second Vatican Council. As *peritus*, Cahal Daly had been intimately and closely involved with the preparation, debating and drafting of the Council's Constitution on the Liturgy at the time. Now he had the responsibility of implementing that same Constitution in his diocese. The ground had been well prepared. His predecessor, Bishop MacNamee, who himself had been present at the debates of the First Session of the Council, had been very committed to liturgical reform and had done much to prepare his people for what was to come. The diocese, as inherited by Bishop Daly, was ready for liturgical change. Many of the churches in the diocese needed renovation. Even the more recently-built ones would have needed the reordering of their sanctuaries for the renewed liturgy. A process of instruction and re-education of laity and clergy was set in train. Study groups and parish councils were set up. The cathedral itself was to prove a major problem.

In the winter of 1961 the artist and sculptor Ray Carroll, who had been a contemporary of Cahal Daly in the Paris student days, set up a small exhibition in his home-cum-studio in a remote valley close to the Pine Forest in the Dublin Mountains. Father Cahal Daly had been one of those who had braved the winter conditions to visit the exhibition. As a result of this visit, the artist soon afterwards found himself in receipt of an invitation to visit Belfast with the aim of discussing the design of a set of Stations of the Cross for the chapel of the Good Shepherd Sisters, to whom Father Daly was then chaplain. The project surprised Carroll who, on leaving Paris and his Socialist colleagues had sworn that he

would never more have anything to do with the Roman
Catholic Church. This despite the advice of the great Jewish
sculptor, Jacob Epstein, with whom he had subsequently
studied: "Go back to Ireland and offer your talents to the
Catholic Church. Work for the nuns; they are great people
to work for."

Now, out of the blue, he was en route for Belfast and a
meeting with a young chaplain whom he did not know at
all, on a project for which, initially at least, he felt no
inclination whatsoever. The journey to the border with
Northern Ireland was not particularly comfortable, hunched
as he was over the wheel of his diminutive Mini Minor. But
worse was to come. At the border he discovered that he lacked
the necessary documentation to take the car into the North.
Undaunted, he parked the car and started to hitch-hike his
way onward.

Two hours behind schedule he arrived at Belfast's Wellington
Arms Hotel to find his host, Father Daly, anxiously waiting.
The chaplain was worried only that something had happened
to the artist. That he had been kept waiting for so long worried
him not at all. The meeting was an important one, not for
the Stations project, which went ahead in due course, but for
the mutual respect and regard that the two found that they
had for one another. It was a business relationship which was
to change, in the course of the years, into a friendship of
collaboration second to none, and one in which the old
doctrinaire attitudes of the French Art student to things
Catholic were to be altered for good.

In 1964 Cardinal William Conway had set up a national Art
and Architecture Committee to help co-ordinate liturgical and
artistic activities throughout the Irish Church. The Committee
met once a month in the National Gallery on Dublin's Merrion
Square, under the chairmanship of the revered Father J. G.
McGarry of Maynooth. One of the members of that committee

was Ray Carroll. On one occasion, when it and a number of other lay committees had met for lunch, Carroll found himself lunching with Cahal Daly. The work of the committee to which Cahal Daly had come having been completed before lunch, Carroll suggested that he might like to sit in on the afternoon session of the Art and Architecture Committee. Cahal Daly readily agreed. Carroll was being devious in this. Some time before, Father McGarry had been removed from Maynooth College to become parish priest in the western town of Ballyhaunis. Now he found that distance impelled him to resign as Art and Architecture chairman. Suddenly, at the afternoon session, Ray Carroll proposed that Father Daly, well known for his interest in liturgical art, should be invited to be the new chairman. There being *nemo contra*, Cahal Daly found himself with a new office, much to his confusion. However, he accepted the position, one which he held for many fruitful years afterwards.

Now, as Bishop of Ardagh and Clonmacnoise, he once again called on his old friend, Ray Carroll. Would he undertake the re-ordering of the sanctuary of Longford Cathedral? It was a bigger task than Carroll had ever undertaken before, but he readily agreed. The process was a long and painstaking one. Not only was a sanctuary to be renewed, but so were many minds and attitudes. There was, among the people of the cathedral parish, a genuine devotion to their church as they knew it. Some of them could see no reason for "messing about with it". What had been painstakingly built and subscribed towards by their forefathers in the Faith should not now be sacrificed in the interest of some new whim.

There followed what some people went as far as describing as a war. The unsuspecting Bishop found himself in contestation with a small but vocal opposition who, when it was discovered that they were, and were likely to remain, a strict minority in the cathedral parish, went on to recruit support from further afield. With patience and determination the Bishop and his clergy set about the establishment of lectures and seminars on the Liturgy Constitution of Vatican II.

The high altar in the cathedral, architecturally inappropriate as it was, also showed serious signs of dilapidation. Foundations had shifted, cracks had developed, even in the table of the altar itself. Pieces of masonry from the Gothic pinnacles were in danger of toppling off with the likelihood of injury or worse to those in the sanctuary below. Restoration, even if it had been a realistic proposition, given that the material of the altar was seriously sub-standard Sicilian marble, would have been at best a short-term solution. But more seriously, the altar was, of course, constructed with its table fixed to the reredos so that Mass could not be celebrated with the priest facing the congregation, as was the prescribed position in the restored liturgy. The altar would have to come down. A new design for the sanctuary was begun by Ray Carroll working in conjunction with two well-known Dublin architects, Wilfrid Cantwell and Richard Hurley. A scale model of the new proposed sanctuary was built and set up in the parish hall for all to see. Consultation was widespread and, thanks to the machinations of the opposition who were operating protest techniques as outlined at that time in the *Observer* newspaper, so was media hype.

The atmosphere was personally very painful to the bishop, who saw himself as ultimately merely striving to implement the prescriptions of Vatican II, and who was firmly convinced that what was being done was for the spiritual benefit of the People of God. The protesters claimed that the decision to change the sanctuary was "undemocratic", an argument which left the bishop singularly unmoved. He knew that the Church of Christ was simply not a democracy. It was governed hierarchically, with bishops, like himself, charged with making the responsible decisions albeit after due consultation, even when such decisions were not universally popular.

A great screen was erected before the sanctuary of the cathedral as the work got under way. Mass was celebrated at a temporary altar placed facing the congregation before the screen. Behind, the old altar was dismantled and slowly the new sanctuary took shape. Crucial to the whole design was an enormous tapestry, twenty-eight feet in height, stretching up from floor level and carrying the colour scheme of the carpet up into the vault of the cathedral apse. With three days to spare to the deadline of Easter 1974, the project was finished and, when the cathedral had been closed for the night, the great screen was removed, the lights were switched on and the sanctuary, in its full glory, was seen for the first time by the Bishop and his clergy, who up to then had only known it through the scale model and from monochrome, one-third size cartoons. "When I saw it," he later said, "I went on my knees and thanked Almighty God. I knew that what had been done was so right." The diocese of Ardagh and Clonmacnoise has ever since served as a model in liturgical renovation for other dioceses and churches throughout Ireland.

In the summer of 1972, a 26-year-old architectural assistant offered himself to the Bishop of Ardagh and Clonmacnoise as a candidate for the priesthood. Sean Casey visited the bishop in his Longford house. Together with his architectural studies, the young man had been reading the documents of Vatican II and had now reached the conclusion that he would have to change course. The meeting went well; the Bishop accepted his offer and Sean Casey embarked on his study for the priesthood at Maynooth where, in the course of the following seven years, his career was followed with paternal interest by his bishop who, on his occasional visits to Maynooth on episcopal business, never failed to call the students from his diocese to meet him in his room at the college. (Each member of the Hierarchy retains a room for his own use in the national seminary.) Sean Casey's organizing abilities meant that the Bishop had him earmarked for special duties from an early date. Yet, the student was surprised and somewhat dismayed to be told, in the months leading up to his ordination in 1979, that he would, after a short holiday, be required to take up duty as his Bishop's secretary.

The promised holiday barely had time to materialize. Plans were to be overtaken by events.

There had been rumours for some time that the Pope, John Paul II, was anxious to visit Ireland. Then, in July of 1979, the decision was made; he would come to Ireland en route for the United States of America, at the end of that September. The Irish Hierarchy immediately appointed Bishop Cahal Daly as their liaison man with Rome. The Bishop sent for his newly appointed secretary and, in the strictest confidence, told him of developments and asked him to curtail his post-ordination holiday and to report for duty at once; there was a lot to be done.

A room was made available to the Bishop in the Irish College in Rome, and Cahal Daly spent most of the following months in that city, dealing with the Vatican and with the Holy Father himself on behalf of his fellow bishops. Rumour back in Ireland suggested that, among his duties, he was to draft sermons and speeches to be delivered by the Pope when he came to Ireland. Cahal Daly, however, always countered such suggestions with a firm: "Nobody writes sermons for the Pope!" Which is certainly true. However, it was widely believed that he was in fact instrumental in helping the Pontiff with background information on Ireland and particularly with regard to the troubled political situation in the North. In the years following the papal visit, those with a bent towards textual analysis claimed to be able to find traces of the Daly style in many of the papal addresses, and particularly in that historic address at Drogheda when the Holy Father spoke directly to the men of violence and begged them "on my knees" to change their ways.

As soon as knowledge of the proposed visit became public, Ireland, North, South, East and West was plunged into a frenzy of activity. There were only a few short months to go and so much to be done.

Within the confines of the diocese of Ardagh and Clonmacnoise there lies the remains of the ancient monastic settlement of Clonmacnoise itself. The Pope had expressed the hope that he would be able to visit one such site. It is well known that Irish monks had travelled the length and breadth of Europe between the fifth and twelfth centuries, bringing with them their knowledge of the gospels and their skills as both preachers and scribes. They had found their way even to the Urals and to the ancient city of Kiev. It was even possible that traces of their presence could be detected in the Pope's own city of Krakow. After some deliberation it was decided that the Pontiff would visit Clonmacnoise and there give thanks for the work of the Irish monks.

Suddenly, the young priest-secretary had a new set of headaches. On the telephone from Rome, his Bishop charged him with setting up the necessary preparatory committees for a papal visit to his diocese. That summer was to be a baptism of fire for the newly-ordained Sean Casey.

The time flew. Within what seemed no time at all it was September. The whirlwind papal visit to Ireland was under way.

The ancient site of Clonmacnoise is a natural amphitheatre on the eastern bank of the River Shannon. There, in the year 545, a young Connaught man with a magnetic personality founded his monastery. It was a cosmopolitan meeting-place, situated as it was where the road to the west crossed the broad-flowing Shannon. It had, through its own internal strength, survived a thousand years, despite the incursions of Viking and Norman invaders who swept up the river in their fleets of longboats. Today, where stand the monastic ruins, the graves and the imposing high crosses, there had once been the wooden huts housing, not only the monks, but also countless students who had come there, lured by the monastery's strong literary tradition.

The green sward of the river bank is dotted with the flat-laid tombstones of the monks who had been buried there between the eighth and twelfth centuries. Still standing are the ruins of the cathedral, centre-point of the monastery, as well as the walls of many smaller chapels. And above all there are the crosses, carved granite masterpieces, prime examples of the narrative sculptors' art. On their panels can be seen depictions of all the main events in both the ancient Jewish and the Christian Scriptures. Towering over all are the two ancient round towers, traditionally both belfries and store-houses for treasured manuscripts.

It was on a blustery day at the end of September 1979 that the monastic silence of the ancient holy place was shattered by the sound of a helicopter's engine. The scarlet-painted aircraft swept in low behind the round towers, a striking visual anachronism. From the throats of the twenty thousand pilgrims who had been gathering there since the small hours, there arose a great cheer of welcome. The Bishop of Ardagh and Clonmacnoise proudly led his special guest across the sward to that spot, before the traditional burial place of Saint Ciaran where, on a specially erected altar, there rested two masterpieces of ancient Irish church art, the crozier of Saint Mel, dating probably from the tenth century and the twelfth-century shrine of Saint Manachan. After a few moments of prayer before the shrine, the Holy Father mounted the specially prepared dais and spoke to the people of Ardagh and Clonmacnoise.

Dear brothers and sisters, This visit to Clonmacnoise gives me the opportunity to render homage to the traditions of faith and Christian living in Ireland. In particular, I wish to recall and honour the great monastic contribution to Ireland that was made here on this revered spot for one thousand years, and whose influence was carried all over Europe by missionary monks and by students of this monastic school of Clonmacnoise . . .

Never forget the wonderful boast and commitment made by Saint Columban to (Pope) Boniface IV in Rome: "We Irish . . . are disciples of Saints Peter and Paul . . .; we hold unbroken that Catholic faith which we first received from you."

And in Ireland today, this Catholic faith is unbroken, alive and active by the merits of Our Lord and Saviour, Jesus Christ; and by the power of his grace we can and must always be this way in Ireland.

In the Holy Father's use of the word "we" instead of "you" in that sentence some claimed afterwards to see a hint that the text might have had its origin closer to Ardagh and Clonmacnoise than to Rome!

Bishop Cahal Daly then presented the Pope with a selection of mementoes of his visit: A copy of *Cluan Chiarain*, a history of the people of the diocese by historian Father John Corkery; an oak-bound history of Clonmacnoise from the monastery of Roscrea and a specially bound copy of Bishop Daly's own book *Peace – the Work of Justice*.

Time was pressing. Nine hundred thousand more pilgrims were even at that moment awaiting the Pope's arrival in Galway and at the national Marian shrine at Knock. With the blustery wind snatching at his scarlet cloak, the Holy Father and his entourage were led once more across the green sward towards the papal helicopter. It was at this point that enthusiasm took over from good order. Reluctant to see their guest depart, the crowd of up to twenty thousand, who had so far remained in place outside the low perimeter wall of the monastic site, decided, one and all, to escort the Holy Father on his way. The small force of local Gardai, who up to that point had had no trouble in controlling the crowd, were now taken completely off guard. They too were enthralled by their papal guest. It was him that they were watching; not the crowd. Suddenly, they were swept aside and the Pope came as close to being mobbed as at any time in his career! Afterwards, Archbishop Paul Marcinkus, celebrated papal "minder" and constant escort of John Paul II on those early papal journeys, said to Bishop Daly with perhaps a hint of ire in his voice: "There's only one thing wrong with your Irish policemen. They are too damn Catholic!"

The papal party made it safely back to the helicopter and, as his guest was whisked away westward, the Bishop of Ardagh and Clonmacnoise could begin to relax for the first time since that day in July when he first knew that the successor of Saint Peter was to visit Ireland.

As in the case of greatness, some people, including bishops, have responsibility thrust upon them. For such, the constant exercise of that responsibility cannot but be a strain. Meticulous dedication to duty together with a tendency, as suggested by his friends and colleagues, to undertake willingly whatever peripheral tasks came his way, meant that Bishop Cahal Daly was always busy. When not immediately concerned with the business of his diocese he would be found engaged in ecumenical activity, chairing meetings, working on one of his many books, drafting documents or one or other task undertaken for and at the request of his fellow bishops. Time and overwork inevitably take their toll. There were also disturbing rumours going round that he was being considered for transfer to the troubled Northern diocese of Down and Connor, vacant now since the retirement of Bishop

William Philbin. Although Down and Connor was, in fact, his native diocese, Cahal Daly felt that by this time he had "grown away" from it. His contacts and his work were all now firmly centred in Ardagh and Clonmacnoise and, really, the troubled Belfast diocese would be a task for a somewhat younger man.

By the end of 1981 he had even got to the point of admitting to his secretary, Father Casey, that he really was exhausted. But there was little prospect of a rest. The work habit had even encroached on his spare time to the extent that his suitcase, whenever he did get away for an annual holiday, was packed with books and papers; items that there simply had not been time to read in the preceding year. Holiday clothing would be strictly limited. Without the books a holiday would not be a holiday!

On February 4th, 1982, Father Sean Casey received a telephone call from Sheila Daly, the Bishop's sister, who was staying with her brother in Longford at the time. The Bishop was feeling unwell. Could he, Father Casey, come to the house at once? The Bishop had been unwell for some days. Despite the attentions of his doctor, the severe indigestion that he was experiencing would not go away. It was decided that hospitalization was the only answer. And it was also decided that, rather than go into the local hospital in Athlone, where there would be little hope of keeping matters quiet, the relative anonymity offered by Dublin's Saint Vincent's Hospital was his choice.

As the Bishop came out of the house to get into the car, his secretary, Father Sean, was genuinely shocked at his aspect. His face had a frightening pallor. The patient was tucked into the back seat of the Renault 20, Sheila Daly chose to ride in the passenger seat in front and Father Casey took the wheel. The journey to Dublin was as swift as the Friday evening traffic would allow. Both the driver and his companion in the front of the car were acutely aware of the increasing discomfort of their passenger. On arrival at Saint Vincent's, the emergency team was immediately on hand. Bishop Daly was whisked away for examination and within half an hour his cardiologist, Doctor Mauer, was back with Sheila Daly and Father Casey. The Bishop was, indeed, at that moment going through a cardiac crisis. They had arrived just in time. For two days the Bishop lay, semi-conscious, in the Intensive Care Unit of Saint Vincent's. Then, on the third day, the danger had passed. Cahal Daly remembered waking up, his mind unexpectedly bright. Suddenly, into his mind there flashed a thought. It was a thought that brought a wave of relief to his whole being; nobody, now, would dare to transfer him to the diocese of Down and Connor! He was safe. Thanks be to God! He turned over and went back to sleep.

He could sleep peacefully then, but God's ways are not man's ways and, within a few short months, while he was still enjoying his convalescence at the family home in Belfast, sure enough, there was to be another call to the Nunciature in Dublin. The Holy Father in Rome wished . . .

Many years later, in a broadcast for the BBC Radio Four programme "Prayer for the Day", he recalled that on this occasion, as on many others, he found himself having recourse to a prayer of Charles de Foucauld:

Father, I abandon myself into your hands;
do with me what you will.
Whatever you may do, I thank you:
I am ready for all, I accept all.
Let only your will be done in me,
and in all your creatures.
I wish no more than this, O Lord.
Into your hands I commend my soul:
I offer it to you

with all the love of my heart,
for I do love you, Lord,
and so need to give myself,
to surrender myself into your hands,
without reserve,
and with boundless confidence,
for you are my Father.

CHAPTER SEVEN

Down and Connor

*Keep your distance from the man
who has power to put to death,
and you will not be haunted by fear of dying.
If you approach him, make no false
move, or he may take your life.
Realize that you are treading among the trip-lines,
that you are strolling on the battlements.*

[ECCLESIASTICUS 9:13]

THE BELFAST-CENTRED diocese of Down and Connor is the second largest diocese in Ireland. It is no sinecure. On a sunny summer afternoon in October of 1982, the new Bishop of Down and Connor took up residence in his diocese. On the first two nights he stayed at his sister's home on Rosetta Avenue, while a mere stone's throw away, the staff at Lisbreen, the official bishop's residence, prepared for his arrival. With them was Peggy Gallogly, who had been his secretary in Longford and who now, in a generous act of personal dedication, was to stay as a guest at Lisbreen for the next five months, so as to introduce the local staff into the pastoral ways and means of their new bishop.

The picture she painted was of a vigorous man, with clear and distinct ideas of his own targets and the means to reach them. A man of great energy and a single-minded sense of purpose. By the time he arrived, two days later, a sense of apprehension had grown amongst them. They even admitted to feeling nervous. But with his arrival, his firm handshake and ready smile soon dissipated all such ill-founded feelings. They liked him from the start.

It soon became clear that for him there was no such thing as a "working day". If necessary, he would work round the clock. But, on the other hand, there was always time for people. No-one was in trouble but he was the first to know, and the first to comfort. There quickly grew up a strong feeling of family in Lisbreen.

Housekeeping and secretarial staff soon learned his ways. He liked to dine alone, usually with the radio to hand, in order to catch up with the day's news. On the other hand, morning coffee or afternoon tea would often be taken *en famille* around the kitchen table. Then there would, more often than not, be laughter. They learned to share his quick sense of humour and his genuine, uninhibited laughter. These meals and snacks would more and more often be interrupted by the telephone. It was a strict principle with him that a call must always be taken, usually right away, often to the desperation of Cook, who saw yet another meal spoiling or going cold while the needs of priest or politician took precedence, yet again.

It was the work that counted. Always. To this end, the new bishop was fascinated with business technology. His staff had to master the science of computers. Not for him old-fashioned typewriters or duplicating machines. A new laser printer would come on the market. Would it improve efficiency? Was it speedier than others? Then get it! Nor would he waste his own time in mastering the technology. His task was to think! The office equipment was for the use of others. His own personal "office equipment" was altogether more traditional. Soutane pockets were often crammed with pencils, pens and ballpoints. When away from home he would buy pens where others would buy souvenirs. And among his greatest treasures was an old wooden ruler that had been his father's in the old schoolmastering days. That ruler travelled everywhere with him. Even to the exalted setting of the Vatican Synod Hall. It was a day of personal tragedy to him when, somewhere en route from Rome, the ruler fell, unnoticed, to the floor of the aircraft. Insistent calls to the airline afterwards failed to recover the treasure and eventually life had to go on with yet another link with the past gone.

Of an evening they would find him striding alone in the gardens, sometimes with his rosary beads swinging from the hands clasped behind his back, at other times he would be quietly humming to himself – more likely melodies from the Eurovision Song Contest than hymns. Even when praying in the garden, he liked to walk briskly. (A visiting nun once said to him: "Why are you going so fast? There's nobody after you!") It was even rumoured that he had asked the gardener to straighten out some of the more meandering pathways, so that he could maintain his speed, even in the dark.

Lisbreen is a red-brick, Victorian villa, standing in its own tree-shaded grounds on the Somerton Road in the northern outskirts of Belfast. For all its peacefulness, its new incumbent had little illusions as to the many tasks lying ahead of him. He would have to preach a Gospel of peace and reconciliation in a community riven with troubles of every kind. Twelve long years of communal violence in Northern Ireland had already passed when the new Bishop of Down and Connor arrived at his new home. Fear and hatred were endemic in the community. The great injustices of the past had been succeeded by the tensions and tyrannies of the present. Christian communities, on either side, were held victims of the self-appointed men of violence. Intimidation was the spectre that haunted every street, every social grouping.

Asked, in a BBC television interview at that time, as to what he could hope to offer such a damaged and suffering flock, Cahal Daly said: "I would hope that people would be able to look to me for understanding of their problems, concern about their problems – proclamation of their problems." And who should hear such proclamation? "Our own more affluent people should hear . . . and should realize what is going on here in our own city – because we are insulated from it far too often."

In this, the bishop was consciously and deliberately identifying himself as part of the more comfortable, middle-class stratum of society with his characteristic directness of approach. He went on: "Many sections of the community are totally insulated from this. They go on with their pretty affluent – their pretty comfortable lives and say, 'Oh those people over there. They are no good. You cannot expect anything from them. They are always like that,' instead of trying to go and see what these people are suffering. They are our brothers. They are our sisters. They are entitled to the same human dignity, the same human rights as the rest of us are . . .We must not think in terms of Them and Us. It is all of us together. We all suffer. When they suffer, we suffer with them – be they Catholic or Protestant.

"Where you have people who are voiceless, feeling powerless, feeling leaderless, feeling frightened and afraid – because they are frightened and afraid they will turn to whoever seems to offer them the most immediate support and help. Often enough, these tend to be the men committed to violence because they are pretty clever at exploiting fear – at exploiting suspicion.

"Now, I think that the Church must be the one to offer, credibly and sincerely, leadership and protection and support to those people, and be their voice . . ."

Very soon it would be understood that fear and intimidation had no place at Lisbreen, nor in the life of the new bishop. Sinn Fein learned to hate him. (It is not too strong a word.) He consistently and vigorously "withstood them to the face", denouncing their injustices and their posing as social reformers. One of his difficulties lay in the fact that, over the years, Sinn Fein had succeeded, to use the bishop's own words, in hijacking most of the schemes for social reconstruction. A counter-attack was what was needed. It soon became apparent to him that one possible solution to the troubles lay in providing employment. "Jobs to combat violence" was to become his slogan, and so was conceived the East Belfast Project, to become known as "Catholics Caring".

Within a very short time, the sum of one hundred thousand pounds sterling, had been raised within the Belfast Catholic business community. This was to be the "seed money" for a series of trusts, grants and other schemes for the setting up of small businesses which, in turn, would provide a continuous stream of jobs for the hitherto unemployed. In addition to finance, the same community was to make available, at no cost, invaluable directorial and management skills.

This was one local enterprise programme that the IRA or Sinn Fein could not succeed in hijacking. Instead they set out to blacken it by attacking it as "collaboration with the Brits", this on the grounds that it was undertaken with the cooperation of the Department of Economic Development, the Industrial Development Board and the Local Enterprise Development Unit, all agencies of Central Government. As far as the bishop was concerned it was a matter of "sticks and stones . . ." Slander was the least of his worries.

Derelict factory and office space was acquired, repaired and refitted. At the beginning of the scheme, unemployment was running at the disastrous level of fifty per cent. There were eighteen thousand unemployed people in West Belfast, with the inevitable social consequences. West Belfast had the greatest concentration of acute social and economic problems of any area in the whole of Ireland. Over a period of fifteen years, leading up to the setting up of the scheme, this situation had never improved; indeed it had steadily worsened. Government had even admitted inability to change the situation. But now, the scene began to change.

A development agency with the name of Worknet was set up. Its brief was to develop the employment and enterprise skills of the community in West Belfast. By means of a series of Job Clubs and a local training programme it aimed to place five hundred unemployed people in permanent employment each year.

By the time Cahal Daly would come to leave Belfast, the entire scheme would be operating at an ever increasing rate, with a budget approaching twenty million pounds. A vision had become a fact and the "bank" of young unemployed, all too easily a recruiting ground for the men of violence, would have been largely eliminated.

In none of this was Cahal Daly operating as a one-man band. Indeed, the very opposite was the case. Instigator he well might be, but he depended totally upon the cooperation of priests and laity in getting his schemes up and running. He saw himself as initiator. It was for others to carry his plans to fruition. His vision of Episcopacy was that of an enabler. His people willingly picked up the traces and the correctness of his vision was again and again evidenced by the success of the various schemes which he initiated. In the BBC interview quoted above he explained his vision. "(The bishop) is not a politician. He has not either the power or the expertise to create political solutions, economic blueprints . . . but he must go on putting statesmen and political leaders in front of their responsibilities as Christians. The Church, in its politicians, is engaged in its Christian task of promoting the Just Society. I am quite certain that violence will not, cannot, be ended until there are shown to be just alternatives peacefully possible . . . In no way can I, as Pastor, talk to men of violence, or anybody else, and say: 'I have a solution.' I have indeed a solution. And that solution is Christ. There is no other. And I will continually believe and teach that if the Gospel of Christ is being lived, then the problems of society will be solved."

Meanwhile, the violence continued. Part of the problem, as seen by the bishop, was the failure of the security forces to maintain that stance of impartiality which would help to establish their credibility and acceptability with the community as a whole. In August 1983, Thomas "Kidso" Rielly was shot dead by a British soldier. He was a young man of twenty-two years of age, from the Ardmonagh Gardens area of the city. By occupation he was road manager for a pop group, travelling with them all over Ireland and Britain. He was a young man with no political involvement and no connection with any paramilitary organization. His killing aroused intense resentment throughout the whole neighbourhood. An immediate investigation was promised and instituted by the British Army.

The soldier in question, Private Ian Richard Thain, who was a mere eighteen years of age at the time of the shooting, was brought to trial in Belfast Crown Court in December 1984. He was found guilty of murder and given a life sentence – the first serving British soldier to be given such a sentence while on duty in Northern Ireland since the troubles began.

The accused claimed that he had fired in self-defence, because, he said, he had reason to believe that Thomas was carrying a gun and was about to draw it. The trial judge found, however, that Private Thain had "concocted the defence", and had been deliberately untruthful when it suited him. The judge said: "This confirms my conclusion that the accused had no honest belief that the deceased was about to draw a gun and shoot him."

The judge said that he had taken into account the soldier's youth and inexperience and the fact that at the relevant time he had been suffering from lack of sleep. Nevertheless, the judge declared that he did not accept that the accused had been suffering from emotional shock or reaction, and pointed out that the soldier had not warned colleagues about the possible possession of a gun by Thomas.

The trial, and the sentence of life imprisonment, seemed at the time to carry the clear message that the security forces personnel were never to be allowed to see themselves as being above the law and were at all times to be, and to be seen to be, amenable to the law of the land in the exercise of their duties. All the greater, therefore, were the amazement and incredulity evoked in the community when it was announced that Private Thain, after serving only three years of his life sentence, had been released on a licence from the Home Secretary; and, more astonishingly still, had been reinstated in his Army regiment. The London *Daily Telegraph* called the whole event an act of "gross insensitivity". In a leading article, this newspaper, normally supportive of the British Conservative Government, went on to say: "What is incomprehensible is the recall of the man to his regiment, an act of such stunning insensitivity that we find it hard to imagine what the Ministry of Defence was thinking of."

This whole episode had to be seen in a much wider context. There had, at the time, been a whole series of events which had seriously harmed Anglo-Irish relations and which had given a serious setback to the credibility of the security forces. The London *Times* linked the Private Thain episode with the Stalker enquiry and the decision not to prosecute RUC officers, in spite of evidence of "perverting or attempting or conspiring to pervert the course of justice or obstructing a constable in the execution of his duty". *The Times* called both these decisions both foolish and wrong. It said, in an editorial: "These misjudgements are wrong, not because they fail to take into account the views of the Republic: they are simply wrong. In addition, they have serious consequences for public faith in the security forces."

Perhaps the most depressing aspect of these events for the bishop was that it seemed that the British Government had not yet grasped that the only way forward out of the stalemate of destruction in Northern Ireland lay in the formulation of a systematic policy for establishing conditions of credibility of the political, legal and judicial institutions of the state, together with a patient and planned policy of building up public confidence that the security forces would be non-partisan, politically impartial and fully answerable to the rule of law. Scant respect for the rule of law was surely shown in the Stalker affair, and similarly scant respect for the courts in the Private Thain episode.

What was needed was the acceptance, by the British Government, that the struggle for hearts and minds was much more important than any purely military success. Internationally, Britain's own reputation was being put on the line. The credibility of Britain's influence and the acceptability of her intervention in disputes elsewhere throughout the world was being undermined. In a sermon, preached in the Holy Trinity Church, on Sunday, 28th February, 1988, and referring to the Thain case, Bishop Daly said:

"I wish to make it clear that I do not criticize the application of reasonable clemency in the case of prisoners. In fact, I am constantly pleading for the exercise of the prerogative of clemency. I have done so recently in the case of the Birmingham Six. I firmly hold these six prisoners to be innocent. I trust that their innocence may be vindicated by appeal to the House of Lords." The bishop went on: "I also believe that the Private Thain decision opens the way to the granting of pardon in their case. It has been said that the exercise of clemency for them would be unjustified, because the appeal judges did not recommend it. There was no recommendation of clemency by the judge in the case of Private Thain, but this did not prevent his release from being approved by the Home Secretary."

(The Birmingham Six were eventually to be cleared and released in 1991, the result of a painstaking campaign by friends and relatives of the Six, and of consistent pressure on the authorities by Bishop Daly and his fellow bishops.)

In the Private Thain case, it had been said that this was a young man who had made "a tragic error of judgement in very difficult circumstances". But, the bishop went on: "One is by no means putting members of paramilitary organizations on the same footing as the members of the security forces when one points out that there are many young men, both loyalists and republicans, who similarly became victims of the tragic circumstances surrounding them in their early and middle teens, and who made ruinous errors of judgement, with disastrous consequences for their young lives and tragic consequences for their victims. Such young people are at least in part victims of a violent society. Society, and in particular, those responsible for political decisions in society, cannot absolve themselves from their share of responsibility for the conditions which allowed or even encouraged these young people to be so calamitously misguided."

He went on to point out that there were still many young prisoners, both loyalist and republican, who were SOSP's, that is to say, they were detained at the Pleasure of the Secretary of State. Many of these had already served more years in prison than would be accounted a "life sentence" on mainland Britain as well as many other countries. In contrast, these young prisoners, and their families, lived from day to day without the slightest indication of how long their sentences would last.

The setting up of a Life Sentence Review Board had been an enlightened and humane measure. Paramilitary organizations opposed the measure and tried to dissuade their members from appearing before the Board. Undoubtedly, they saw in it some threat to their influence over the prisoners. In spite of this pressure, however, prisoners continued to appear before the Board. Nevertheless, the paramilitary leaders were soon able gleefully to say to the prisoners: "We told you so! We told you the Review Body was a sham, and now you see for yourselves that we were right." The many apparent inconsistencies in the decisions of the Board gave this retort plausibility with the prisoners. The Review Board, which had been intended to bring hope into the lives of Life Sentence prisoners, was now perceived by those same prisoners to be as likely to bring them despair and disillusionment as to bring hope.

A joint working party of the Irish Catholic Commission for Justice and Peace and the Irish Council of Churches, in a study of the problem, called "Punishment and Imprisonment", recognized that many such prisoners "in different circumstances . . . would be unlikely to run foul of the law". Some of them were scarcely youths when they became caught up in the net of violence, their naive and youthful idealism having been exploited and manipulated for the perverse purposes and methods of an ideologically motivated "cause". Prudent acts of clemency, conducted in a responsible, systematic and sustained manner, would be a recognition of the collective responsibility of society, and particularly those in charge of the political policies and institutions of society, for the conditions in which violence began and had been perpetuated.

In the same homily, the Bishop went on: "Our society is desperately in need of a change of heart. A change of heart cannot be forced. But it can be evoked. Only mercy can evoke mercy. Clemency and mercy are not simply Christian virtues, they can also be forces for political change and for social transformation. There are political and legal implications in Saint Paul's analysis of the decadent state of Roman society in his time. When he speaks of men who have come to be 'without honour, love or pity', he speaks to our condition too. Saint Paul can find no escape from 'this body of death' except in 'the grace of God through Jesus Christ, Our Lord'.

"But," the Bishop went on, "let it be remembered that in Christian history 'grace' became a legal term as well as a theological one. The grace of God, given to all of us through Jesus Christ, was held to call for answering human 'grace' even within the legal and penal system. Hence the traditional concept of 'the King's Grace' and 'the Queen's Grace'. This legal concept has a biblical basis, as had so much else in the Common Law tradition. I believe that a prudent policy of conscious clemency towards prisoners would make a significant contribution towards countering paramilitary propaganda and reducing support for paramilitary organizations, and towards the hope of reconciliation and peace in our bitterly polarized society.

"Finally, I renew my Lenten plea to the whole Catholic community to ask the Lord to help us to pull out anger and bitterness from all hearts by the root. Let us bring political as well as personal angers and hurts to Christ, in order that they may be healed. Let us become, in thought and emotion, in speech and in action, men and women of peace, so that the peace of Christ may find acceptance in our lives and in our land."

Justice must not only be done; it must be seen to be done. Failures in this gave rise to a real sense of anger, not just in the Catholic community as a whole, but in the heart of their bishop in particular. It could be allayed, at least in part, by his conscious and deliberate expression of his feelings in the calming atmosphere of the Christian liturgy.

The degree to which the bishop felt he could be outspoken in his dealings with the British authorities, even when he was being critical of them, meant that they, in their turn, could take him at his word. A senior civil servant once said: "We always felt that we understood him, and that he understood us."

Through the success of the Catholics Caring programme he succeeded in opening important doors for Catholics at Stormont. Whenever he spoke, politicians and civil servants listened and took action. His name and his suggestions were something to be taken very seriously indeed; a situation that brought with it advantages and disadvantages. He was able to establish an excellent relationship with Richard Needham, later to become Northern Ireland Minister of State for Industry, and with Tom King, Westminster's Northern Ireland Secretary.

On one occasion, a number of classrooms at the school in Saint Peter's parish fell into disuse. In the official jargon of the Department of Education, they became "surplus to requirements". As such, their conversion to other use lay strictly in the hands of the Department, who, in the estimation of the bishop, were unlikely to agree to such a conversion, at least for quite some time. Father Matt Wallace, Curate at Saint Peter's, suggested to his bishop that they would be ideal to house the parochial Job Club, an organization which he was setting up to enable unemployed youngsters from the area to meet prospective employers. The bishop agreed. Other unused classrooms could be used as a base for his Adult Education programme. When they heard of these proposals, the officials at the Department of Education were horrified. It couldn't be done. It was outside their remit. There was no precedent for such action. What would happen if such a precedent were now to be set? The objections were endless. Cahal Daly said to Father Wallace, who was dealing with the Department on his behalf: "Tell them this is what the bishop wants. If they want to discuss things further, they can approach him directly." They never did. The Job Club was established in the classrooms and went from strength to strength. In all such matters, his priests found that Cahal B., as they called him, would back them and their efforts for their people one hundred per cent.

The fact that the Bishop could deal openly and frankly with the authorities at Stormont, often securing not only agreements for projects, but on occasion, funding too, was a matter of great frustration to the IRA and their supporters. They knew that any monies secured by the bishop for his projects always went entirely and solely to those projects and could never find its way into the coffers of those who dealt in bombs and bullets.

Hence their continuous denunciation of him and his works as puppets of the British Government. Their answer, however, was given by one grateful West Belfast parent: "If it wasn't for Bishop Daly, West Belfast would still be out in the cold."

He himself often said: "Direct political discussion is no part of the Church's mandate. But this is not to say that the Church has no political role." He liked to quote Karl Barth who said that every true sermon must be in some sense political because religion has to do with the whole nature of society.

CHAPTER EIGHT

Seeds of Violence

The rage of the wicked man cannot justify him,
for the weight of his rage is his downfall.
The patient man will hold out till the time comes,
but his joy will break out in the end.

[ECCLESIASTICUS 1:22–3]

Susan Daly (née Connolly),
Cahal's mother.

Charles Daly, Cahal's
father.

Charles and Susan Daly.

The six Daly children
(*back row from left*, Cahal, John,
Nicholas; *front row from left*, Margaret
Mary, Rosaleen, Sheila.)

Daly the Queen's University
student, with relatives in
Loughguile, 1936.

Daly attired for his gradua-
tion ceremony as Bachelor of
Arts, Queen's University,
Belfast, July 1937.

LEFT: Ordination year, 1941.

BELOW: Lourdes, June 1961, with sister Margaret Mary (who died in September of the same year), her husband, and a classfellow, Fr Gerald Laverty.

ABOVE: On the day of Daly's
ordination as Bishop of
Ardagh and Clonmacnoise,
14th July 1967.

RIGHT: With handicapped
children, 1969.

BELOW: The restructured
sanctuary of Longford
Cathedral, first revealed at
Easter 1974. *(Bishop Colm O'Reilly)*

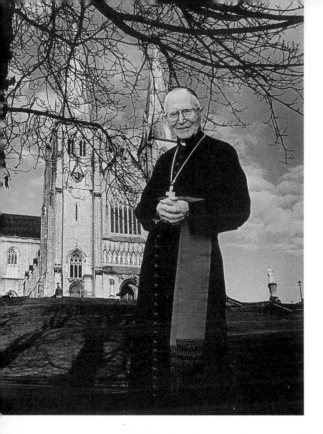

Archbishop Daly in front of St Patrick's Cathedral, Armagh.
(Robert Allen Photography)

BELOW: With the Pope at Clonmacnoise, 30th September 1979. Cardinal Tomas O'Fiaich, the then Primate, is to the right of Bishop Daly.

ABOVE: The Pope greets
the new Cardinal.

LEFT: Cardinal Cahal B.
Daly today.

THE TROUBLES, or at least the most recent manifestations of them, for they are essentially an historical entity, began as early as 1967, with the first rumblings of a young Free Presbyterian minister by the name of Paisley. There followed the early manifestations of Loyalist violence and the 1968 "battle" of Burntollet Bridge, when a peaceful civil rights parade was beset and stoned. From then on, those who would have "supported" the civil rights movement with more than peaceful marches were only too ready and willing to rally to the cause. The result was that complex concatenation of events leading into that spiral of violence in which Northern Ireland has been entrapped ever since.

It is the unfortunate fate of any Christian minister in Ireland, North or South, that he has to tangle, at some stage or another, with the problem of violence, its effects, and those things that give rise to violence in the first place. This is true no less for bishops than for anyone else. Those days are gone (if ever they existed) when a bishop could retire to his ivory tower, or his palace, and administer his diocese vicariously whilst praying, albeit sincerely, for the wellbeing of his clergy and flock. Irish bishops of the late twentieth century do not live in such a world.

Thus it was that, from the time of taking up office in Belfast, all Cahal Daly's preaching on peace matters, particularly on occasions such as the annual celebrations of the Day of Prayer for World Peace was centred on the Northern Ireland situation. This was a vital issue and had to be addressed. "If the Church were not seen to be speaking clearly on the Northern Ireland Troubles", he said "then our credibility as a Church would be severely questioned." The result, as far as Bishop Cahal Daly was concerned, was the articulation of the most clear and distinct exposition of the Church's teaching on the legitimate and illegitimate use of violence. It may well have been that there were other clerics whose hearts were so deeply affected by the sufferings of the Catholics of Northern Ireland that their prayers and attitudes could be, and sometimes were interpreted as, being at least ambiguous with regard to the use of force by the Provisional IRA and others. Not so with Cahal Daly. There was a clear line to be drawn and a clear doctrine to be preached: Injustices there were. Injustices must be rectified. But that rectification must be carried out by all legitimate and constitutional means. The established political machinery was there to be used and legitimate authority was to be challenged where such challenge was justified, but never by violence, particularly by those who would arrogate to themselves the choice as to whether to wield the ballot box or the bullet, and the right to destroy human life.

While he was Bishop of Ardagh and Clonmacnoise, the troubles north of the border were at somewhat of a remove. It has often been said, and with some justification, that those who live in the Republic, no matter how deep their concern over events in the North, never really and fully understood what was happening up there, let alone how the matter could ever be resolved. This would never have been true of Bishop Daly of Ardagh and Clonmacnoise, however, for although his entire diocese was in the South, was he not, himself, a son of the Antrim Glens? Were not his mother, sister and brother still living in Belfast? Did he not spend much of whatever spare time he allowed himself with his family in Belfast? Thus his statements on the Northern situation, even when stationed in the Republic, were always accepted as the words of someone who fully "knew what he was talking about". When, however, he had to return to Belfast as its bishop, then the matter was different. Now he was in the midst of things. Now it was "his own" people who were suffering. Now those sufferings came even closer to his own heart.

Despite those "firm line" statements on the illegitimacy of both Republican and Protestant violence, in the face of that violence the new Bishop of Down and Connor suffered greatly. He saw it as an essential part of his episcopal ministry to be with those who suffered bereavement even though, as he said himself, "sometimes there is nothing I can do except to be with them and to weep with them". And weep with them he did. Often and deeply. During his eight years in the diocese of Down and Connor he personally officiated at over forty funerals of people who were the innocent victims of violence, whether paramilitary or other. These were either "revenge" killings of Catholics by Protestant paramilitaries or "accidental" killings of Catholics by Sinn Fein or the IRA. He regularly visited the homes of bereaved wives and mothers whose young men were killed in the "armed struggle" where those womenfolk sincerely, as was so often the case, had no idea that their sons or husbands were involved with the paramilitaries. He would only do so, however, where there was not the slightest danger that his visit might be construed or portrayed as being some kind of act of support for the so-called "armed struggle". Similarly, the sensitivities of the situation were such that he would never visit the homes of Protestant victims where his visit might in any way constitute an embarrassment for the family. Nevertheless, he often did visit such homes and was greeted with the greatest of kindness and appreciation. Again, he was often at a loss for words, never at a loss for tears, and those tears were, as often as not, a more eloquent expression of sympathy than any word could have been. Did he find such visits difficult, he was asked. "No, not at all. There is no difference between Catholic grief and Protestant grief, between Protestant and Catholic tears."

Again and again in these situations he spoke of how he was struck by the spirit of courage and forgiveness shown among the families of those who had been killed. And as long as there was such courage and forgiveness to be found there was also hope. That hope was to sustain him throughout his ministry.

Although there were those, from his earliest days in Down and Connor, who would try to persuade him to talk with the men of violence, particularly Sinn Fein's Gerry Adams, Cahal Daly resolutely refused to do so. He could not and would not consider any personal contact with such people until such a time as they would forswear the use of arms and accept the ballot box as their only weapon.

The closest contact he had with the perpetrators of violence were the many pastoral visits which he made to the prisons in his diocese, the Maze, McGavery and Crumlin Road. Often the prisoners would have been forewarned of his coming and would have prepared their briefs in order to confront him. Again and again he was to feel that particular sense of frustration at his being unable to get through to them at the level at which they were thinking themselves. It seemed to him that although their logic was irrefutable, their arguments started from the wrong premises. Their reading of history and of contemporary political reality was completely flawed. They relied on out-dated Marxist dialectical principles; the implacable opposition of Left and Right. They had never clearly defined their own version of Socialism, nor had the courage to put it before the people for discussion and reflection. It seemed to him that they had never grasped the total inconsistency between their "military" struggle and their political campaign. There were glaring self-contradictions. They had never realized, or allowed themselves to realize, that the eventual success of the 1916 Dublin uprising (to which they consistently appealed in justification of their own actions) was due, not to the fact that it had ended in military victory; militarily it had been an unmitigated disaster, but to the fact that it had captured the popular imagination country-wide, and thus had made the continued British presence impossible. It was the political, not the military, aspect of the Dublin uprising that won the day, eventually securing the political independence of the greater part of Ireland. This view he put to the prisoners again and again and it utterly defeated him and frustrated him that they could not see that their movement's utter failure to obtain wide popular support in Ireland, North or South, was an absolutely glaring proof of their political failure. Sinn Fein had never put forward for popular consideration a feasible, realizable political programme. At the same time, their military efforts (both those that they would claim as successes, resulting in the loss of life among the armed forces or amongst British politicians in England or Northern Ireland, or "errors" in which they sacrificed the lives of innocent people, Irish or British) had deprived them of any possible political credibility.

His failure to convince those he visited in prison of the error of their ways was a constant sorrow to Cahal Daly. It did, however, reaffirm him in his conviction of the urgency of providing jobs to occupy young minds and bodies before they could fall foul of the indoctrinations of the various paramilitary-backed youth movements. And at an even earlier stage, there was the question of education.

The old Jesuit slogan, give me the boy and I will give you the man, was never more surely endorsed than in Northern Ireland where the various Churches guarded carefully those educational agencies which, under the Northern Ireland educational system, were allocated to them. Both Catholics and Protestants guarded jealously those schools which were rightfully theirs and have never been willing to surrender their proprietorial rights.

As soon as he arrived in Down and Connor, the new bishop was faced with the problem of the schools. There was a lobby which protested that all interdenominational conflict had its root and origin in the school system and that therefore a valuable first step would be in eradicating denominational schools altogether and establishing interdenominational schools throughout the province. Neither the Catholic nor the Church of Ireland (Anglican) hierarchies accepted this point of view, even when, in due course, a group of concerned parents set up one such school, Lagan College, with Government backing.

Writing, with the Reverend Eric Gallagher, in "Violence in Ireland: A Report to the Churches", Bishop Daly said:

> The question of an "integrated" system of education is being increasingly canvassed and cannot be passed over in silence . . .We are in agreement that the Churches should promote pilot schemes and research projects to find effective ways of bringing together Protestant and Catholic young people at school level. Such schemes could include exchanges of teachers between Catholic and Protestant schools . . .Shared Sixth Form Colleges have been suggested. Common nursery schools in suitable areas could be developed . . .
>
> The teaching of religion in schools of both traditions must have explicitly and deliberately an ecumenical dimension. The stereotypes which each community may have inherited regarding the religious beliefs and practices of the other must be firmly rejected and replaced by exact and sympathetic understanding. ("Violence in Ireland. A Report to the Churches", Daly & Gallagher, Veritas Publications, Dublin, 1976, 1977.)

There is, of course, no direct consideration here of the possibility of wholesale integrated schooling. But Bishop Daly, writing in 1979, firmly puts the case against, quoting not just the Churches but the educational establishment itself. The passage merits quoting at some length:

> "Integrated schooling" is one of the most commonly urged "solutions" for the Northern problem. This is a complex question and is frequently over-simplified . . .
>
> The British Government's Green Paper of November 1973 . . . referred to the question in the following terms:
>
>> One of the obvious factors in the whole situation is the high degree of educational segregation. This is not of itself in any way peculiar to Northern Ireland. The importance which, in the United Kingdom and in many other countries, certain of the Churches place on their own school systems stems from deep conviction about the need for an underlying religious basis to all teaching. While, in Northern Ireland, it is the Roman Catholic Church which maintains a separate system, it is by no means to be assumed that, in practice, all Protestant parents would be happy to see a completely integrated school system . . . (H.M.S.O, 1973.)

The Bishop went on to quote from Dr James Russel's work on the same topic:

> Given the high likelihood that parents and religious leaders will object to their children being taught by Orangemen or Republicans indiscriminately, integration (of schools) may simply involve the two-way movement of pupils and teachers without pupils being taught by someone of the opposite religion. Such a situation could involve playground battle-scenes that could make street riots appear as minor incidents.

The consequences of forcibly using integrated schooling in an attempt to unite different communities, without community cooperation, will probably end by driving them further apart. The problems connected with creating mixed housing areas and/or bussing pupils and teachers with different religious complexions may provide confrontations and different levels of intimidation as yet unseen in Northern Ireland . . .

Further on, Russel called attention to the divergent expectations in respect of "integrated schooling":

Protestants may see it (integrated schooling) as a means of getting rid of Catholic schools and inculcating loyalty to Northern Ireland, thus ensuring the predominance of their way of life. Catholics, on the other hand, may see integrated education as a good means towards economic advantage, conversions of Protestants through marriage, and eventual absorption of the Protestant community into a United Ireland. ("The Sources of Conflict", Dr James Russel, in *The Northern Teacher*, 1974.)

In invoking such an "outside" authority, the bishop reinforced the traditional Churches' opposition to the suggestion of integrated schooling, at least as a simple answer to the pains of Northern Ireland and the situation has not materially changed since, although educationalists on each side have courageously and often successfully undertaken mixed projects, as suggested above, with an increasing degree of success. Busloads of schoolchildren regularly cross the border in both directions en route to "integrated" educational and recreational projects of whose value there is not the slightest doubt.

Sometimes linked with the pressure for "integrated schooling", the Bishop went on, in the same work:

. . . is the demand for relaxation of the Catholic Church's

regulations on inter-Church marriages or "mixed marriages". The Catholic Church has in fact introduced important changes in her legislation in this matter. *The celebrated "Ne Temere" decree has been revoked.* (Author's emphasis.) This one fact seems often to be overlooked, particularly in the fulminations of the more vigorous anti-Catholic propagandists, it being more convenient for them to ignore the important change of attitude that such revocation has indicated.) Since 1970 the Church's requirements are those formulated in the *Motu Proprio, Matrimonia Mixta.* This certainly did not satisfy Protestant wishes in respect of inter-Church marriages; but it is important to recognize just how genuine was the Catholic Church's desire to detect and to remove what caused offence to Protestants . . .

In virtue of the 1970 legislation, no promise, whether written or verbal, is now asked from the Protestant partner. The Catholic is asked to recognize and acknowledge that he, as a Catholic, has a grave obligation from God to do all in his power to have all his children baptized and brought up as Catholics. This is the only reason why a promise is required now, and it is required of the Catholic only. The Church is surely not exceeding her right here . . .The Church's attitude can never be understood if it is interpreted in political or demographic or sociological terms. It is a question of doctrine, of ecclesiology, of how the Church understands herself . . .

There is neither justification nor excuse for the use of emotive slogans, such as "religious genocide", which have sometimes been put in circulation. Concern for the future of the Protestant population of the Republic would urge that factors other than mixed marriages would have to be given due attention. Undue concentration on the mixed marriage factor alone could prevent the search for remedies for the other factors.

It is intriguing to note that researchers agree that mixed marriages have no demographic importance in Northern Ireland. The population problems of Protestants in the Republic seem linked to and inseparable from their being numerically a very small group and a proportionately very small percentage of the total population, artificially cut off from the preponderantly major portions of their respective church communities in Northern Ireland. These problems are also found to be independent of the comparatively favoured economical position of Protestants in the Republic. If this is so, then the complex factors producing a decline in the Protestant population may prove to be the inevitable consequences of the partition of Ireland.

The bishop concluded, not hesitating to speak, in this, not just for himself, but on behalf of the entire Hierarchy, saying:

> We bishops would most earnestly wish it to be accepted that it is reasons of conscience, and reasons of conscience alone, which have guided us in our thinking and our practice in respect of inter-Church marriages. We are anxious to do everything that conscience allows, in dialogue and cooperation with other Churches, to make the problems of mixed marriages less hurtful to relations between the Churches and less painful for the partners of inter-Church marriages. (Cahal B. Daly, "Peace the Work of Justice", Veritas Press, Dublin, 1979.)

It would eventually fall to Bishop Daly to formulate and defend the position of the Irish Hierarchy and the Irish Catholic Church when he, together with his episcopal colleagues the Bishops of Clonfert, Derry and one of the auxiliar bishops of the Archdiocese of Dublin appeared before the New Ireland Forum in February 1984.

CHAPTER NINE

Facing the Forum

*Reason must be the beginning of every
activity, reflection must come before every undertaking.
Thoughts are rooted in the heart
and this sends out four branches;
good and evil, life and death,
and always mistress of them all is the tongue.*

[ECCLESIASTICUS 37:16–18]

TOWARDS THE END of 1983, the then Primate of All Ireland, Cardinal Tomas O Fiaich, received an invitation from Professor Colm O hEocha, of University College, Galway and Chairman of the New Ireland Forum. The invitation was to make a submission, on behalf of the Roman Catholic Church in Ireland, to that Forum.

The New Ireland Forum had been set up earlier that year and held its first meeting in Dublin Castle on May 30th. It had been set up in order to carry out consultations on the manner in which lasting peace and stability could be achieved in a new Ireland through the democratic process.

The Forum was open to all democratic parties which rejected violence and which had members elected to the Irish Oireachtas (Legislature) or to the Northern Ireland Assembly. Four political parties took part; Fianna Fail, Fine Gael and Labour from the Republic and the SDLP from Northern Ireland. Thus the Forum was roughly representative of seventy-five per cent of the Irish population and up to ninety per cent of the Nationalist people of Northern Ireland. The members of the Forum met in 28 private sessions and thirteen public sessions. Written submissions were invited from interested groups, both north and south of the border. As a result they received 317 written submissions following which 31 groups were invited to follow up with public oral presentations. One of the most important of the groups which responded was the Irish Episcopal Commission.

The bishops, meeting at Maynooth, appointed their delegation and set about drafting their submission. The *Chef de Delegation* was to be the Bishop of Down and Connor, Cahal Daly. The other members were Dr Joseph Cassidy, media spokesman for the Hierarchy, Dr Edward Daly, Bishop of Derry, Dr Dermot O'Mahony, Auxiliary Bishop in Dublin, who was both a civil and canon lawyer and President of the Irish Commission for Justice and Peace, and Reverend Michael Ledwith, Secretary of the Bishops' Commission for Ecumenism. (Mr Matthew Salter, Lecturer in Education at Queen's University, Belfast, and Professor Mary McAleese, Reid Professor of Criminal Law at Dublin's Trinity College would later join the delegation for their public, oral hearing at the Forum.)

The delegation, under the presidency of Cahal Daly, set about drafting their submission, which eventually reached the Forum in January 1984. In it, they pointed out that the bishops had shared the agony which the violence of the previous fourteen years had caused to the whole people of Ireland. They had prayed and worked unceasingly for the restoration of peace and were longing for the day when a just solution would be found to the outstanding problems. By their repeated denunciations of murder, kidnapping, destruction of property and other crimes as contrary to the law of God, they had kept constantly before the people the sanctity of human life and the Christian duty of loving all men and women as children of God. Yet, they confessed, with the leaders of the other Churches, they had so far failed to secure their overall objective of a just and lasting peace. Thus, they regarded the Forum as a valuable political initiative in that it served to raise the hopes of many at a time when a long succession of failures had given rise to a considerable sense of frustration.

They recognized, or course, that since the Forum was in the nature of a political instrument, any contribution or input made by the bishops would inevitably be limited. They would consider it inappropriate, for instance, that they should make any recommendations regarding possible political structures or arrangements.

But insofar as it was impossible to deny that there was a religious dimension to the Northern conflict, their submission would confine itself to certain religious or partly religious topics which might have a bearing on the solution of the problems.

These came under five broad headings: Ecumenism, The Family, Pluralism in its various forms, the Alienation felt by Catholics in Northern Ireland, and the Catholic School System.

As a result of their written submission, the bishops were then invited to send their delegation to a public meeting of the Forum to take place on Thursday, February 9th, 1984.

Saint Patrick's Hall, in Dublin Castle, is a splendid place, the setting for great national occasions, such as Presidential inaugurations and state receptions. On February 9th its deep blue carpets and the cream and gold decor of its walls and pilasters gleamed in the brilliance of the television lights. For without doubt, the public appearance of the Catholic Church's delegation before the Forum was seen as an important national occasion and was being carried, live, on RTE, the national broadcasting service.

Bishop Cahal Daly, briefcase in hand, led in the members of his delegation to a buzz of anticipation from the press and those members of the public who had succeeded in obtaining tickets for the small number of seats in the public gallery.

The Chairman of the Forum, Professor O hEocha, rose and

warmly welcomed the delegation and invited Bishop Daly to open the proceedings.

"The Catholic Hierarchy," he said, "ardently desires to promote lasting reconciliation and justice and peace in Ireland and so it welcomes the efforts being made by the New Ireland Forum towards achieving these aims. Any failure in its efforts would, in our view, be a grave setback to hopes for a just and agreed settlement to our island's grievous problems. Those working to bring about a reconciled society in Ireland will not find the Catholic Church an obstacle in their path."

There followed what was to be welcomed as one of the key statements of the session; one that was to have repercussions well outside the walls of Saint Patrick's Hall:

The Catholic Church in Ireland totally rejects the concept of a confessional state. We have not sought and we do not seek a Catholic State for a Catholic people. We believe that the alliance of Church and State is harmful for the Church and harmful for the State . . .The Catholic Church in Ireland has no power and seeks no power except the power of the Gospel it preaches and the consciences and convictions of those who freely accept that teaching. The Catholic Church seeks only the freedom to proclaim the Gospel. It proclaims the same doctrine and moral message under whatever constitutional or political regime operates in this island. The Catholic Church has always carried on its mission on the basis of a Thirty-two County Ireland. Since 1922 it has promulgated exactly the same teaching in Northern Ireland as in the Republic of Ireland. Political considerations cannot determine the fulfilment of a trust that we believe that we have received from Christ. We are acutely conscious of the fears of the Northern Ireland Protestant community. We recognize their apprehensions that any political or constitutional or even demographic change in Northern Ireland would imperil their Protestant heritage . . .We do here and now declare, and declare with emphasis, that we would raise our voices to resist any constitutional proposals which might infringe or might imperil the civil and religious rights and liberties cherished by Northern Protestants.

This statement was greeted by a spontaneous and prolonged burst of applause from all present. Its importance as a statement and proclamation of good faith was both recognized and appreciated but not, as it turned out, immediately or by everybody. The report of Cahal Daly's statement, made as it was, publicly and in the name of the whole Hierarchy, was widely publicized. News of it soon reached the ear of the Reverend Jack Weir, at the time Clerk of Assembly and General Secretary of the Presbyterian Church in Ireland. He and Bishop Daly were firm friends, having together represented Northern Ireland at meetings of the European Council of Churches. Each had a healthy respect for the other, recognizing in each other able debaters and doughty champions of the respective causes. He was currently engaged in a speaking tour of the United States of America. During a public question-and-answer session he was asked by a newspaper reporter for his reaction to the statement of Bishop Daly in the Forum on the defence of Protestant rights and liberties. To which he replied: "I am sure that the Bishop means what he says. But I am not sure that we (Protestants) would see it that way if it happened." This riposte, inevitably and in due course, was relayed to Cahal Daly when he had returned to his home in Belfast. The Bishop was deeply wounded at what he saw as an attack on his sincerity and veracity. He wrote at once to the Reverend Weir expressing his personal hurt at what he said. On his return to Ireland, however, jack Weir hastened to contact the Bishop and soon all misunderstandings were behind them and their friendship was once again restored to full health.

A not unimportant aspect of the appearance of Bishop Daly

and his colleagues at the New Ireland Forum was that it presented an opportunity for the Hierarchy, through its delegates, formally to give to the Forum and to the Irish people a fresh presentation of truths which had often before been expressed but largely in the form of written statements of considerable length, often as either joint or individual Pastoral Letters. These letters, by and large, had retained the style and vocabulary of the nineteenth-century Church, and as such, could scarcely have been described as popular reading.

Procedure at the Forum was mainly through the simple expedient of dialogue, the members of the Forum being asked in turn to address the Church delegation and ask them questions which, in a court of law, would certainly have been regarded as "leading". Nevertheless, in the context of the Forum they were no more than a convenient method of eliciting important information.

The opening question was put by Mr Seamus Mallon of the Northern Ireland Social Democratic and Labour Party. Inevitably, it was on the topic of violence. He asked whether the Hierarchy would regard the campaign of violence being waged by the Provisional IRA as being a misuse of physical force?

The reply, from Cahal Daly, was brief: "Totally, unequivocally, unreservedly, and we have said so from the very beginning of the campaign."

Mallon went on: "In your opinion then, any political party which advocated the misuse of that political force, could not . . . claim acceptance merely on the basis of political pluralism?"

"Absolutely," said the bishop. "The political party in question has gone on record as saying that it demands from all its candidates and members unequivocal support for what they call the 'armed struggle'. Therefore, everyone who supports and who votes for that party (the party in question being, of course, Sinn Fein) must realize that their vote is certainly going to be misrepresented as a vote for violence. That is a very, very serious responsibility to assume in conscience."

There followed an expression of concern and understanding that was to recur often as the proceedings developed:

"Having said that, I must also say that many people are driven, because of frustration, because of the alienation, the sense of exclusion, of hopelessness and the conviction and, from their point of view, the experience, that constitutional politics has not been permitted by the institutions of the State and has not been able to make political progress, to the conclusion that there is no hope of political change. They are duped into voting for (Sinn Fein). But they must realize, and experience is there to show it, that their vote will be interpreted – whatever their intentions – as a vote for violence."

This sense of frustration on the part of Northern Ireland Catholics, it was explained by Bishop Edward Daly, of Derry, was due to the fact that direct rule of Northern Ireland from Westminster, introduced as a temporary expedient, had led to fourteen years of life where there was government without consensus and "so many things happening over which you have no control".

Seamus Mallon asked for clarification on a final point: Was the armed struggle as defined by Mr Gerry Adams of Sinn Fein morally correct?

Cahal Daly answered again: "Unequivocally and in the most emphatic terms I declare in the name of the whole Episcopal Conference that it is totally unjustified, immoral. I would also like to say . . . that it is totally defeating the very aims it proposes to set itself to accomplish. Our great need in Ireland is for reconciliation between divided communities. Violence drives the communities further and further apart." The Bishop sat back in his chair, happy that he had been able, in such direct terms, to proclaim one of the most fundamental and important teachings of the Irish Hierarchy in recent times.

The meeting of the Forum continued throughout the morning with the other members of the delegation setting out the Church's teaching and point of view on divorce, civil and ecclesiastical, marriage, both in-Church and inter-Church, ecumenism, education and, repeatedly, the sense of alienation felt by Northern Ireland Catholics.

One of the Labour representatives that morning was a young constitutional lawyer and barrister, Senator Mary Robinson. She asked whether, in view of the Hierarchy's conviction that the introduction of civil divorce in Ireland would be a direct attack on the very institution of marriage and the family, and in view of the fact that that conviction was not shared by the other Christian Churches, whether a constitutional prohibition of divorce could be justified in a New Ireland? To which Cahal Daly replied: "We know very well that there are marriage breakdowns in Ireland . . . that they are increasing and that some remedy must be found. Surely it should not be impossible for us in this country with our tradition to find alternative provisions, to find other ways than simply slavishly copying the one that is nearest to hand, the divorce legislation that obtains in other jurisdictions. Surely it should be possible, within our own values and traditions, to look for other ways that will alleviate the very real cases of tragedy which need compassion, and to do this without undermining the stability of the family and weakening the moral consensus on which the whole stability of society depends."

It was unlikely that either the Bishop or the young lawyer to whom he was responding foresaw, at that time, that within a matter of half a dozen years, he would be greeting her, as President of Ireland, at his solemn installation as Archbishop of Armagh.

As the session was drawing to its close, Mr John Kelly, an elected member of the Dail, Professor of Roman Law at University College, Dublin, and a distinguished barrister, rose to question the delegation on the separation of Church and State: "Would the delegation recognize that the Government's duty is a duty to act on its own judgement, even where its collective judgement might differ from the judgement or perception of the Church to which perhaps the majority of its members, perhaps even all its members, might individually belong?"

Bishop Daly replied: "Yes, politicians are dealing with a separate set of criteria . . . and these have to be put into the balance along with the moral criteria which we, as our pastoral duty, lay before our people who include the legislators in some cases, but include also a proportion of the people of the country."

A little later, John Kelly asked a question of Bishop Daly that was to give rise to one of those good humoured exchanges which were a characteristic of the whole encounter. On the possibility of their being a change in the Irish Constitution which would remove the constitutional ban on divorce: "Could I ask whether we can take it for granted that the Church at least would not throw its weight into the scale if there were a move to . . . bring the Constitution of this country back to what it was in the years 1922 to 1937 when there was no constitutional bar on such enactment, and years in which it can scarcely be argued the country was less Christian than it is now?"

The Bishop replied: "I am afraid, with very great respect, I would feel that that is a political question which is not appropriate for us to answer."

Kelly: "It is not a political question, but I do agree that it is probably the first time since Saint Patrick arrived that the representatives of the Hierarchy were asked to think on their feet." His remark was greeted with a burst of that laughter that sometimes leavens and lightens such occasions and in which Cahal Daly himself joined.

And John Kelly went on, as the season drew to a close: "I should like to thank the delegation, again, for their great frankness and their willingness to submit to an unprecedented interrogation from lay people."

One thing remained for clarification, however.

Cahal Daly asked: "May I have just one short final word? It is in connection with the discussion we had earlier about the morality of voting for Sinn Fein and its connection with the morality of violence. I feel I should put it on record. There has been some question about a division of opinion between the Cardinal (Cardinal O Fiaich), for example, and myself. This, emphatically, is not the case. We both say, and we say unambiguously, that it is morally wrong to support violence or to vote for political parties which support violence. This we will go on saying . . . It is simply not true; it is false and fraudulent for Sinn Fein to seek votes on social and community grounds and then turn around and claim that the votes so sought and so obtained are votes for violence. In the great majority of cases they are not. This gives Sinn Fein a specious but an utterly spurious and dishonest claim to electoral support for the Armalite (rifle).

"We have welcomed the opportunity of coming in person to meet the members of the Forum . . .We sincerely thank all of you, the members, for your time. We admire your dedication and your commitment. Might I even say, without wanting to preach at the end, that we assure you of our prayers, such as they are. We are grateful to you for allocating so much time to this presentation. Thank you."

These thanks were reciprocated by the Chairman, Professor O hEocha, on behalf of the members of the Forum and the session closed at exactly ten minutes to four in the afternoon.

A pale winter sun was shining across the castle yard as Bishop Cahal Daly led his fellow delegates down the great staircase and out to find a refreshing cup of tea, content that a valuable day's work had been done.

Many years later, when asked for his assessment of the Forum Bishop Daly was quite clear; the great achievement of The New Ireland Forum lay in the very fact that it represented that pan-national consensus allegedly sought for by Sinn Fein who themselves were self-excluded from that consensus by their endorsement of violence. And they would continue to be excluded from it until such a time as they would give up their support for that violence.

CHAPTER TEN

The Roman Synod

For conversation seek intelligent men.
Let all your discussions bear on the Law of the Most High.
Have virtuous men for your table companions,
and let your pride be in fearing the Lord.

[ECCLESIASTICUS 9:15–16]

THE SECOND VATICAN COUNCIL had closed on December 8th, the Feast of the Immaculate Conception, 1965. It was the end of one of the great Church events of the twentieth century. As the world's bishops, together with their *periti*, packed their bags and headed for home, they knew that, whatever else lay ahead, it was unlikely that they, as a group, would ever reassemble in such circumstances again. The organization of an ocumenical council is a mammoth undertaking and, although there is no rule to say how often a council should be called, many of them felt that it might well be another century before Vatican III or its equivalent could realistically take place.

Nevertheless, the work initiated by the Council could not now be allowed to grind to a halt. There had to be some way in which the momentum generated could be sustained for the immediate future. For this very reason, Pope Paul VI, who had "inherited" the Second Vatican Council upon the death of Pope John XXIII, called for the establishment of a permanent consultative body of bishops for the universal Church. It was to be perpetual and, by meeting regularly with the Holy Father, would ensure continued close communication and collaboration between him and the bishops of the world. And so it was that what came to be known as the Synod of Bishops was established and "built into" the final decree of the Second Vatican Council. The departing bishops now knew that there would be a continuous working contact between Rome and themselves. The Synod would meet every three or four years and would enable the work of Vatican II to be continued in such areas as evangelization, ministry in the Church, catechetics and any other topic which needed dealing with at any time. On three occasions Bishop Cahal Daly was to be a member of the delegation to the Synod representing the Irish Hierarchy, in 1977, 1987 and 1990, although, curiously, always as a substitute either because of the death or the illness of an episcopal colleague.

The purpose and workings of the Roman Synod have, as often as not, been misunderstood, possibly as a result of the over-simple media criticism that it was a "mere talking-shop, without any executive power". From the beginning of his involvement in the Synod, Bishop Daly quickly felt that this was an altogether false criticism. He saw the Synod as a most effective exercise of episcopal Collegiality.

Collegiality, both as a doctrine and as an attitude, is one of the important notions to have been developed during, and as a consequence of, the Second Vatican Council.

The doctrine is that all bishops have a corporate responsibility, not just for their own dioceses, but for the unity of faith and of communion within the universal Church, this arising from their shared ordination and from their special communion with the Roman Pontiff.

The attitude arises directly out of this. It is seen in that spirit of mutual cooperation with one another on the international, national and regional levels. An example: in earlier years it had not been unknown for individual bishops to be extremely possessive in the matter of their priests. They "belonged" to them and not to anyone else. Under Collegiality, however it is much easier, and much more frequent, for any individual bishop with a serious staff problem to "borrow" or even have transferred permanently, by mutual agreement, the clergy he may need.

That aspect of collegiality most notable during the actual meetings of the Synod at Rome was, in Cahal Daly's experience, the extraordinary way in which Pope John Paul II spent so much of his working day simply listening to what his bishops were saying. The Pope personally attended almost every General Session of the Synod, (the Synod meets in General Sessions and in smaller Language Groups). Not only that, but every papal meal during the Synods was, and is, a working meal. The Holy Father invites either individual delegates or, at times, small groups of common language or common interest to share breakfast, lunch and supper with him. On several occasions, Bishop Daly was to have the pleasure of attending such meals and noted, once again, the sheer informality with which they were carried out. The Pope was as anxious to have his guests speak out as he was to speak himself. "We all felt that what the Pope was showing us was his real need of personal contact with us. He needs to know us and to know of our problems and our successes." In this way, John Paul tried to meet, at least once, every working delegate at every session of the Synod.

Given the history of often exaggerated reverence for which the Papacy was noted, particularly in recent centuries, at least up to the time of Pius XII, who never ate in company and whose only table companion, it was said, was his pet canary, this exercise of Papal hospitality is something more than a curiosity. It represents a change and development in the working and the theology of the papacy.

During the 1987 Synod, which was devoted to discussion of the place and ministry of lay men and women in the Church, selected lay delegates from around the world were invited to address the Holy Father and the assembled bishops. For three whole working days the synod hall was at the disposal of the laity. John Paul listened with that intensity which had become a hallmark of his participation.

Both Bishop Daly of Down and Connor and Cardinal O Fiaich, who were representing the Irish bishops at that session, were gravely disappointed to find that no member of their Pastoral Councils had been invited. Even the officers of the Irish national Laity Commission had been overlooked. However, not to be daunted, they, on their own authority, sent for them and arranged for them to be accommodated at the Irish College. Bishop Daly himself was at Fiumicino Airport to greet them as their flight arrived and was often at their door before they had risen, in the mornings that followed, to brief them on the synodal business of the day ahead and, before long they too had their admission passes to the synod hall and their chance to meet the other delegates. Nevertheless, it remained a deep regret to both Cardinal and Bishop that those whom they wished to be present were not invited to be official delegates.

Another meeting of the Synod was held in the autumn of 1990. Once again, Bishop Daly of Down and Connor was there, alongside Archbishop Desmond Connell of Dublin, as the Irish representatives. It was during this session that Cahal Daly was to receive news of yet another change in his episcopal career. The Archdiocese of Armagh had been vacant since the sudden death of Cardinal O 'Fiaich in Lourdes, the previous May. There had, of course, been the usual speculation as to who would succeed to the vacant see. Both Bishop Daly and Archbishop Connell had featured in the rumours. Each knew this and each, undoubtedly, prayed that the other might be the chosen one. Neither of them particularly coveted the position; Cahal Daly ruled himself out both on the grounds of age (he was rapidly approaching his seventy-fifth birthday on which, in canon law, every bishop must tender his resignation) and on the grounds of health. He had had, after all, quite a serious heart attack. Surely Armagh would be a task for a younger man! Archbishop Connell, on the other hand, was indeed younger, but as a relatively recently appointed archbishop, felt that a mere two years in Dublin could hardly have provided him with sufficient experience, yet, to make him a candidate. Nevertheless, he had heard the rumours and they were certainly strong enough to cause him worry.

Then came an invitation. Cardinal Gantin, of France, whose brief is the supervision of the world's bishops, invited Cahal Daly to concelebrate Mass with him in his private chapel at San Callisto, and to have breakfast with him afterwards. This was not unusual. The cardinal made sure to have one or other of the synodal delegates with him each morning, and he and Cahal Daly had been acquaintances for many years, having met during some of the bishop's many visits to Paris. Daly, therefore, was not suspicious. Not until, at least, after breakfast, the Cardinal said: "I have an important message for you from the Holy Father." That was enough! He was ticketed for Armagh. The dismayed bishop outlined his well rehearsed arguments of health and age. "The Holy Father has considered all that, my dear bishop, and nevertheless he wishes you to accept the appointment. He will tell you so himself within a few days."

The bemused bishop returned to the Synod but, understandably, could not concentrate on his work. He was, as is customary, under a bond of secrecy and so could not even seek the solace of his confrères. He decided to call it a day, left the Synod and returned to his lodgings at the Irish College where he spent much of the remainder of the day in the chapel, coming to terms with his Lord and with his latest vocation.

There were to be two other fateful breakfasts that week.

Archbishop Connell received an invitation from the elderly French cardinal and, not knowing what had transpired with Cahal Daly and thinking, therefore, that Armagh was still vacant, confided his deep concern at getting the invitation to his colleague from Ireland. Cahal Daly, although still bound by confidence, applied a charitable interpretation to his restriction as far as to say, smilingly, to the younger man: "I think you may accept the Cardinal's invitation with an easy mind." That was all.

The other invitation was to the Vatican Palace. Pope John Paul with his usual informal courtesy told Cahal Daly of his decision to appoint him to the See of Armagh. Once again, the bishop, with deference, pointed out the problems. Once again the Pope listened courteously and then said: "I have thought much about what you say. And I have prayed about it. Nevertheless, I am sure that it is the will of God that you should go to Armagh." There is, of course, no answer to the "will of God" argument – particularly when used by the Pope! There was nothing for it but to accept. Next stop, Armagh.

Once again, he found a ready prayer on his lips; this time a prayer of Thomas Merton:

My Lord, God, I have no idea where I am going.
I do not see the road ahead of me.
I cannot know for certain where it will end.
Nor do I really know myself,
and the fact that I think I am following Your will
does not mean that I am actually doing so.
But I believe that the desire to please You
does in fact please You, and I hope that I have that desire
in all that I am doing.
I hope that I will never do anything apart from that desire.
And I know that if I do this
You will lead me by the right road

though I know nothing about it.
Therefore I will trust You always.
Though I may seem to be lost and in the shadow of death
I will not fear, for You are ever with me
And You will never leave me to face my peril alone.

CHAPTER ELEVEN

The Red Hat

*My son, be gentle in carrying out your
business and you will be better loved than a lavish giver.
The greater you are, the more you should behave humbly,
and then you will find favour with the Lord.*

[ECCLESIASTICUS 3:17–18]

THE EVENING OF THURSDAY, June 27th, 1991, was a warm and balmy one. The sun, which had blazed down on the city of Rome all day from a clear, blue sky, had now begun to lose its heat. A fresh gentle breeze was blowing through the trees on the Gianiculum Hill just to the south of the Vatican. Beneath those trees, in the garden of the Villa Spada, the home of the Irish Ambassador at the Holy See, people were beginning to gather for a party.

Ambassador Padraig de Paor and his wife, Mary, were hosting a reception for the cardinal-elect, his family and friends. It was an informal affair. Archbishop Daly and a few *Pezzi Grossi* from the Vatican were there in full episcopal regalia, as was only fitting, (he in episcopal purple for the last time; tomorrow it would be the scarlet of a cardinal). Others were less formally attired. Members of the Irish community in Rome mingled with those who were there for no more than that special weekend of celebration. Priests and layfolk from the dioceses of Ardagh and Clonmacnoise, Down and Connor and from Armagh had come to be with their former pastor at the most special moment of his episcopal career. Tomorrow they would observe the ceremony of the Consistory from something of a distance, but tonight they could stand in the garden of the embassy and share a drink and a snack with him in total informality.

The great and the not-so-great rubbed shoulders around the swimming-pool. *Taoiseach* Charles J. Haughey with Foreign Minister Gerry Collins had diverted the Government jet from its planned itinerary from Dublin to Brussels for an EC meeting on the following day to be there, with Ireland's official representative, *Tánaiste* John Wilson. The family of the cardinal-elect stood diffidently to one side as he was engaged in conversation by the elected leaders of Ireland on the very edge of the full swimming-pool. The atmosphere was sufficiently informal for one politically sensitive reveller to wonder aloud whether one small step to the rear might not prove interesting for a *Taoiseach* "on the brink". (His party had recently lost heavily in local elections.)

The gentle murmur of polite embassy-garden conversation was occasionally overlaid by more genial exchanges as old colleagues, lay and clerical, some of whom would not have met for twenty or thirty years since their days of academic studies in Rome, recognized one another and renewed acquaintances. Nor was this a wholly Irish occasion; Bishop Charlie Burns from Scotland, now of the Vatican Archives, was seen earnestly trying to impress a couple of American prelates with the virtues of Bushmill's Black Label. (They, reputedly, had not even realized that there was such a thing as "Irish Scotch"!)

As the evening progressed, members of the Irish media, newspapers and broadcasting, arrived, a little weary from their official briefing at the Palazzo San Carlo, headquarters of the Vatican Council for Social Communications. They too were soon exchanging reminiscences of other similar occasions with old Roman friends. Some of them had had their first encounters with these circles during the Second Vatican Council. Others were veterans of the various Synods and other Vatican ceremonies which had had significance for the Irish in more recent years.

Throughout, the cardinal-elect was quite obviously totally relaxed and enjoying the occasion to the full. If there was any tension or anxiety about the ceremonies of the morrow, there was certainly no trace of them in Archbishop Cahal Brendan Daly.

The sky had darkened and a huge yellow moon hung over the Eternal City before the last limousines and taxis left the gates of the Villa Spada for the various colleges and *pensiones* where the Irish would snatch a few hours of sleep in preparation for the events of the next day.

Warm sunshine greeted the crowds as they began to assemble in the great piazza of Saint Peter's the next morning. Well before eight o'clock, Vatican police and Swiss Guards, in their traditional multi-coloured uniforms, were shepherding long queues of people through the labyrinth of wooden barriers which inhibit direct access to the basilica and the surrounding buildings ever since the failed attempt on the pontiff's life at the beginning of his pontificate. Touring coaches and taxis converging on the Vatican had to tussle with the normal Roman rush-hour mayhem. The air was filled with the hooting of frustrated motorists, the shrill whistles of the traffic police and, occasionally, the urgent wailing of police or ambulance sirens.

The various colours on the entrance tickets thrust at the guards had little significance, as all comers were filtered through the same frustratingly narrow, one-person-at-a-time gaps in the barriers, everyone converging not into the basilica of Saint Peter itself but to the huge modern audience hall, the Paul VI Auditorium, which stands to the left of the great basilica behind the collonades of Bernini.

The auditorium itself is a miracle of modern architecture.

Designed by the celebrated Italian architect Gianpaulo Nervi, its curved floor and ceiling enclose the seven thousand pilgrims, seated, with never a pillar or column of any sort to obscure the view of the broad platform on which so many modern papal ceremonies take place.

To the painful frustration of many, some of whom had only arrived by charter flight from Belfast at four o'clock that morning and who were close friends of Cardinal-elect Daly, it was found that the Vatican authorities had issued far more invitations than the capacity of the auditorium would allow. Realizing this, in the days before the ceremony, the authorities had erected a giant television screen within the basilica of Saint Peter's itself. Thus, many who had travelled so far and had hoped to be present at the Consistory now had to be content with watching the ceremony at second-hand on television. There were even those who, through a marvel of Vatican mismanagement, for which, it must be stressed, the new cardinals incurred no blame whatsoever, failed to gain entry to Saint Peter's, one such being the devoted attendant and chauffeur of the last three Irish cardinals, John Ward who, despite a lifetime of service, was forced to remain outside in the *piazza* in the hope of getting a glimpse of his new employer at the end of the ceremony. There was something a little ironic too in that such an important religious event was to take place in the essentially secular setting of an auditorium while the sacred space of one of the most celebrated religious buildings in the world was reduced to the status of a television theatre!

Meanwhile, inside the vast hall, preparations were continuing. To the accompaniment of soft organ music, the cardinals-to-be, wearing their scarlet robes of office for the first time, took their seats in the front row of the auditorium. Behind them were many members of the hierarchies of the various countries from which the new cardinals had been chosen. Alongside were the members of the diplomatic corps and behind them again, forming by far the greatest part of the congregation, the many thousands of pilgrims from all over the Catholic world for whom this day would be an unforgettable occasion.

In front of them on a raised dais was the papal throne and, to one side, to the right, the College of Cardinals who would soon welcome their new brothers into their number. Opposite, on the other side of the papal throne, were twenty-three empty chairs, to which the new cardinals would eventually be led.

At seven minutes past eleven, uncharacteristically behind schedule, to the sound of a quietly executed fanfare on the organ, John Paul II, Bishop of Rome and Supreme Pontiff, entered with his aides from the left of the platform. Wearing a claret-coloured cape over his white soutane and red ceremonial stole with symbols of the apostles Peter and Paul, his pace was slow and firm, his long strides contrasting with the now quite markedly stooped shoulders.

The sound of the Sistine Choir rang out in a setting of Psalm 32: "Rejoice in the Lord, all ye people. Praise him with the sound of cymbals. Sing unto him a new song." And then the Holy Father began the ceremony in the name of the Father and of the Son and of the Holy Spirit.

In a brief address, he invited all present to pray with him for those to be raised to high office.

Then the tall figure of Archbishop Sodano, the most senior of the cardinals-to-be, moved forward to the lectern. In December 1990 he had been appointed as the Vatican's Pro-Secretary of State, the equivalent of Prime Minister. He was known to have played a vital part in the shaping of the papal response to the imminence and actuality of the Gulf War. The Pope's letters to President Bush and to Saddam Hussein before the outbreak of that war had carried his "imprint". He had also visited Hungary, Romania and East Germany on behalf of the Vatican during the period of rapid change in East

Europe. He had twice visited the Kremlin for talks with President Gorbachev, which led directly to the Soviet leader's visit to the Pope in 1989.

It was his task now to address the Pope in the name of his colleagues, to thank him for his trust in them and to promise him their loyalty.

There followed a brief collect, prayed by the Pope:

Heavenly Father, who in the New Covenant inaugurated by Christ your Son, continue to gather your people from all the nations of the earth in the unity of the one spirit, grant that your Church, faithful to its mission, may always share the joys and hopes of humanity, and may show itself the leaven and soul of the world, so as to renew in Christ the community of peoples and transform them into your family. We ask this through Our Lord, Jesus Christ, your Son, who lives and reigns with you and the Holy Spirit, world without end, Amen.

Then came readings from the First Letter of Saint Peter and from the gospel of Saint Mark providing the theme of humble service which the Pope then developed in his homily.

He reminded them that the scarlet colour of their new robes was no mere convention; it signified the very blood in their veins and he told them that they must be prepared to shed that blood if at any time it became necessary for Christ or his Church.

This was no matter of mere histrionics. There were present before him men, some of whom had already suffered very much for their faith; Archbishop Alexandru Todea of Romania, a priest of the Byzantine-Romanian Rite who in 1951 had been arrested, tried and condemned for breaching the strict anti-religious laws of the Communist regime in his country. Of the group of fourteen arrested on that occasion, he was one of only three to come out of prison alive.

There was also Father Jan Korec, a Jesuit Father from Czechoslovakia. Secretly ordained in 1951, a year after the religious orders had officially been suppressed in that country, he had worked in a factory and as a librarian until in 1960 he was discovered and sentenced to 12 years' hard labour for having ministered to his fellow workers.

And, of course, there was the ninety-year-old Ignatius Kung Pin-Mei of China. As Bishop of Soochow since 1949 he had been arrested by the authorities in 1955 and had spent thirty years in prison, his only crime being that he was a Catholic bishop. The Holy Father had secretly made him a cardinal as long ago as 1979, while he was still in prison, although his name was never promulgated for fear of causing him further suffering. He had been released from prison as recently as 1985 but had been kept under such intense surveillance by the police that his life became impossible and he had gone into honourable retirement in the United States of America.

"You, dearly beloved new cardinals," the Pope went on, "will be the attentive servants and apostles of the Church, associated to my singular Petrine ministry with a new, more direct title. Your special task will be to love Christ, bear witness to him, and make him loved; to love the Church, defend her and make her known, so that all tribes, tongues, peoples and nations may acknowledge that in her the salvation of God is fulfilled to the farthest ends of the earth . . ."

When all had proclaimed together the Apostles' Creed, Cahal Brendan Daly of Armagh and his fellow cardinals pronounced their solemn oath:

I, Cahal Brendan Daly, Cardinal of the Holy Roman Church, do promise and swear that from this hour, for as long as I shall live, I will be faithful to Christ and his Gospel and obedient to Peter and the Supreme Pontiffs of the Holy Roman Catholic

Church, . . . I will fulfill my duties with the greatest diligence and
may Almighty God assist me.

Then, one by one, the new cardinals mounted the platform
and knelt before John Paul, their brother bishop. One by one,
they felt the gentle pressure of his hands upon their heads as
he placed on them first the scarlet *zuchetto*, or skullcap, and
then the three-peaked biretta. At exactly 12:27 p.m. Cahal
Brendan Daly knelt before the Pontiff and at the same moment
the Holy Father assigned to him the Roman church of San
Patrizio or Saint Patrick which is in the care of the Irish
Augustinian Fathers and which, from that moment, became
his titular church in Rome.

Rising to his feet, the new cardinal moved to greet the older
members of the Sacred College with the Kiss of Peace, and
then took his new seat at the side of the papal platform.

Last of all to reach the Holy Father, and walking on the arm
of an assistant, although independent of the wheelchair to
which he is normally confined, came the venerable Kung Pin-
Mei. As the heroic ninety-year-old Chinese knelt before the
Pope, the whole congregation rose to its feet in an
unprecedented and wholly unliturgical gesture to accord him
a standing ovation.

Another short prayer, followed by the Papal Blessing and
it was all over. Outside in the square, the midday sun
heightened the vivid scarlet robes of the new cardinals. Families
and friends jostled to greet them and to take the inevitable
photos. The Czech cardinal was seen to join his traditionally
costumed flock in a folk-dance as they swept him through the
piazza.

The celebrations among the Irish were less exuberant, but
no less joyous. Cardinal Daly accepted the embraces and
congratulations of his family and friends as all made their way
back to the coaches that would take them to their celebratory

lunch. The Consistory was over. Ireland once more had its own cardinal. It was yet another new beginning for Cahal Brendan Daly.

Another new beginning, perhaps, but it was the same Ireland that he had left, to which he flew back at the end of that eventful week. Even as he was leaving Rome, the English Catholic weekly *The Tablet*, under the heading "Angry Irish", was describing the country to which he was returning. " . . .Not only has he to contend with the tensions, divisions and endemic violence of Northern Ireland, which he has been facing so courageously for so long and which will press in upon him in his primatial see of Armagh as relentlessly as they did during his years in Belfast. He has to deal also with the 'extremely high degree of dissatisfaction' felt by Irish Catholics towards a Church judged to be obsessed by rules, distrustful of the laity, male-dominated, authoritarian and narrow-minded."

The quotation was from an opinion poll recently carried out all over Ireland by the very Augustinian Fathers whose Rome church was now the new Cardinal's titular church! "Those interviewed professed a strong faith in a personal God and gave a special place to prayer in their personal lives."

The Tablet went on to quote from Dr David Stevens, Assistant Secretary of the Irish Council of Churches, claiming that Roman Catholic young people were "much more critical of their Church than their Protestant counterparts", and claiming to find "a growing problem for the Church within the Catholic community in the sphere of personal morality issues such as contraception and what to do about family breakdown".

It was unlikely, then, that there would be much of a "honeymoon" for Cardinal Cahal Daly.

Postscript

ON SUNDAY, MARCH 25th, 1990, Bishop Cahal B. Daly of Down and Connor was invited by the minister and congregation of Knock Methodist Church, in Belfast, to give an address. It was to be given as part of a series of special church services arranged to herald the new decade of the 1990s.

The packed congregation heard the bishop deliver a talk which in its broad historical sweep, as well as its theological and scriptural content, went to the very heart of the problems which bedevil life in Northern Ireland.

His message was one of hope in the face of circumstances which so often seem to offer nothing but despair. It was the personal expression of a vision that, in a way, sums up his entire episcopate.

He called it: My Vision for the 1990s.

"Where there is no vision the people perish"; so ran a familiar translation of Proverbs (29:18). The Jerusalem Bible Translation somewhat disconcertingly translates: "Where there is no vision the people get out of hand". The cynic might retort, "when there is too utopian a vision, or too exclusivist a vision, the people get out of hand". Perhaps indeed this has been one of our temptations in Northern Ireland: each of our divided communities has had its own vision, pursued its own aspirations, to the exclusion of the other community's vision and aspirations; each has implicitly or overtly located its own utopia in a place free of the disturbing presence of the other. A united Irish nationalist Ireland with no British presence; a united British and unionist Ulster with no Irish or nationalist dimension – both "visions" have been pursued with fanatical dedication and often through the blood and tears of others down many decades of our history. One person's "vision" has been another's nightmare. Surely we need a broader and more inclusive and shared vision. Surely we must move away from narrow and exclusive visions. In a different context William Blake in a famous couplet said:

May God us keep
from single vision and Newton's sleep.

The prophet Joel, quoted by Peter in his Pentecost Sermon, said:

Your old men shall dream dreams
and your young men see visions (Joel 3:28; cf. Acts 2:17)

No longer young, I am in doubt as to whether what I want to say to you this evening is vision or dream; but whatever it be, I wish to share it with you.

Vision For Ireland

My first vision is for our own land, this island which is our common home. History has brought it about that two religious, political, even in some sense two national traditions share this island together. But surely this fact must now be seen in the light of a divine providential plan whereby God wishes to work out his purposes for both communities. God works in mysterious ways, turning history into providence, fate into gracious invitation and opportunity, place and time into grace. "Everything is grace", said the French writer, Bernanos, quoting St Thérèse of Lisieux.

It has been said that we choose our friends, but God chooses our neighbours. The geographical juxtaposition of Catholic and Protestant, unionist and nationalist, loyalist and republican, and the historical interaction between the two, are an invitation and a challenge to us from Christ to fulfill in a unique way his first and greatest commandment, his new commandment, to love one another as he has loved us; to love one another first, as he loved us first, even when we are enemies; to love our enemies and so by loving them, to turn them into friends.

We have come through twenty-one years of murderous conflict, which has left large parts of our two communities more physically separated, more politically polarized, more emotionally hurt and more mutually untrusting than for many decades. Some look back nostalgically to the years before "the Troubles" as to a kind of golden age and dream of a return to the peace and stability of that time. Yet, without wishing to hark back to ancient wrongs reciprocally inflicted or to reopen old hurts mutually suffered, we have nevertheless to ask whether the apparent peace of that time concealed beneath a complacent surface tensions and tremors which were later to erupt in violence. Perhaps we were saying "Peace, peace", when there was no peace (Jeremiah 6:14), because there was no deep healing, no deep-going mutual caring (Jeremiah 8:15).

Do we pine for the peace before "the Troubles" because it was "our" peace, peace on our terms, stability, normality, order and prosperity, on terms favourable to "our community"; and we in all good faith assumed that what was good for us was good for "them", for "the others", too – be "the others" the

Catholics, the Protestants, the unionists, the nationalists, the unemployed, the badly housed, the homeless, the poor, or whatever. We just did not think of them; it did not occur to us to ask them. We did not seek opportunities of listening to them. Our vision did not include them. They were not "part of us".

The bitter lesson of twenty years has surely taught us that we cannot go back and should not wish to go back to such a time or such a state of mutual non-caring and non-listening coexistence. We must go forward from there. We must enlarge our vision. "The others" are our brothers and sisters in Christ. We are their "keepers". Peguy, in a phrase pregnant with many meanings, once asked:

> What will he say to us if we come back to him without the others?

Whether Protestant or Catholic, we profess in our Creed our belief in the "holy, Catholic Church". The word "Catholic" connotes a fullness, a wholeness, a comprehensiveness of vision. We Catholics are surely being summoned now to include Protestant spiritual insights in our own way of being Catholic. Protestants are being summoned to include Catholic spiritual insights in their way of being Protestant. The respective communities are being called to respect unionist feelings, interests and rights in a nationalist perspective, and nationalist feelings, interests and rights in a unionist perspective. We are being invited to rejoice as Catholics in Protestant faith and Christian witness and holiness of life and praise God for them and be humbly eager to learn from them. We are being invited as Protestants to rejoice in Catholic faith and Christian witness and holiness of life and praise God for them and be humbly eager to learn from them.

If we live in more comfortable and prosperous surroundings,

in peaceful suburbs, associating mainly with our own class and kind, let us not forget the poor and the unemployed, be they Catholic or Protestant, in the Shankill or up the Falls, in Ballymaccarrett or the Short Strand or the Markets, in Forthriver or Ardoyne, in Skegoniell Avenue or Tigers Bay or New Lodge. For the most part, and in their great majority, they do not choose violence, they are its victims. Intimidation, racketeering, hijacking of cars and houses, riots instigated by paramilitaries, heavy-handed security force presence, fear of tit-for-tat random sectarian murder, these are the stuff of everyday life in many areas, Catholic and Protestant. We must not opt out. Through personal and community caring, through social work, through influencing our milieu and wider public opinion, through political involvement, whether as active party members, or in active public life, we must work to serve the total community and make our proper Christian contribution, each in his or her own place, to promote that just and fair and caring society where none feel excluded, all feel wanted and respected, and all are given reasons to believe in peace and to believe in peaceful politics as the only way to justice.

Vision for a more European Ireland

My vision secondly is for a more outward-looking and more European or "Euro-conscious" Ireland. We have been and continue to be too parochial, too inward-looking, in our vision. A new Europe is being formed before our eyes. The iron mould in which the shape of Europe seemed to have been fixed for all foreseeable time has been dramatically, even miraculously, broken. Surely that constitutes both a rebuke and a challenge and an inspiration and a source of hope to us.

Whatever be the eventual configuration of this new Europe – and there are many uncertainties and grave risks ahead – France and Germany will certainly play a vital role as continental axis of the new Europe. When one thinks of the hostilities and hates and hurts which divided these two peoples, the cemeteries across Europe which hold the victims of their blood-lettings in three wars within seventy-five years, and now sees them make common cause in the construction of a new Europe "without frontiers and without wars", one must take hope for the ending of or conflict too. One great symbol of French resistance to the historic German enemy was Verdun. For half a century Verdun stood as a great emotional monument to French national pride and patriotic sentiment.

Yet a few years ago President Mitterand and Chancellor Kohl were able to stand beside one another at Verdun and shake hands in a common pledge to renounce war and work together for a future of peace.

Relationships between the divided communities in Northern Ireland and between Northern unionists and the rest of Ireland, relationships between the Republic of Ireland and Britain must not remain unaffected while relationships all over Europe are being transformed. Unionists should see the value and importance, in European terms and indeed in historic terms, of improved relations between the Republic of Ireland and Great Britain. That historic quarrels and misunderstandings between these two island neighbours should be replaced by mutual trust and cooperation cannot but be good for all of Ireland and would be in line with what is happening between ancient enemies on the continent and between East and West in Europe. Indeed it could serve as a model for other areas divided by memories of ancient wrongs. Selfish concerns should not prevent people in Northern Ireland from welcoming and encouraging these improved relationships.

Nationalists should accept and respect the sincerity of unionist attachment to the Union and its institutions and symbols and of unionist loyalty to the Crown. Nationalists must accept the right of people whose home is Ireland to feel themselves British and to cherish their Britishness. Nationalists should not rejoice in unionist discomfiture or humiliation and should recognize the genuineness of their apprehensions about their future. To replace one community's alienation by the other's can bode no good for either. Unionists should accept and respect the sincerity of the nationalists sense of Irishness and the depth of nationalist commitment to the ideal of a united Ireland, achieved by peaceful means. They must recognize the sense of hurt and wrong felt by nationalists at being regarded as disloyal because they are Irish and being treated as second-class citizens in their own land. If committed Christians, "children of light" (Luke 16:18) whose calling is to walk in the light (1 John 1:7) and to live in love (1 John 4:16) fail to work to earn the trust of other committed Christians and to trust them, from where can light and hope come to our troubled land? God loves and accepts us as we are, loves us while we are still sinners (Romans 5:8); and by loving us changes us. We must love others as they are, accept them as they are, not demand that first they change and then we will love them. Even if we want others to change we must begin by loving and accepting them in their differences.

In the Europe which beckons us as we approach 1992 Northern Ireland and the Republic of Ireland have common interests and shared needs; we have similar difficulties to overcome, similar opportunities to grasp. We have everything to gain from cooperation and partnership. Political differences need not impeded this cooperation. Political convictions should not and need not be compromised by it. Let us not draw back from a path which is for our mutual benefit because of fear as to where it might lead. The slogan "Sinn Fein" means "ourselves alone". There are unionist versions of it as well as nationalist versions. There are unionist "Sinn Feiners" as well as nationalists ones. Such attitudes must be re-thought in the context of Europe. We can still be ourselves while cooperating with others. Indeed "ourselves alone" must be replaced in both communities by "ourselves with the others". Surely that is also the Christian way.

Vision for a more Christian Ireland

Thirdly my vision is for a more Christian Ireland. Pope John Paul has called Catholics to a decade of evangelization as we enter the 1990s and prepare for the end of the twentieth century and the beginning of the third Christian millennium. We Christians know that there is "no other name under heaven given to men and women by which we can be saved" except the name of Our Lord Jesus Christ (Acts 4:12). The only hope but the sure and certain hope for this land of ours is that we turn to Jesus Christ and make him truly our personal Lord and Saviour and the Lord of our country and our century.

We have seen historic miracles in recent months worked in Christ's name. What has been happening in Eastern Europe has indeed demonstrated that he truly is the Lord of history. The revolution which has swept across Eastern Europe from the Urals to the Baltic has been largely the fruit of a primary spiritual revolution. Its prior cause has been the marvellous and indeed miraculous revival of Christian faith and its triumph over atheistic Communism after seventy years of anti-religious indoctrination and savage religious repression. I asked an exiled Soviet dissident recently what, apart from the grace of God, was the explanation for this extraordinary revival. He replied: "Apart from the grace of God, there is no explanation. It is a miracle of grace." Marxist-Leninist Communism collapsed, not primarily because of its economic failure but because of its spiritual bankruptcy. It ceased to provide a system of values and beliefs which could offer a basis for social cohesion or offer reasons for living, for working or for making sacrifices. It could not satisfy man's moral and spiritual needs. To adapt Marx's own words and use them against himself, the "cry of the oppressed creature" was not for communism but for Christ.

The resurrection of Christ is not just an event of past history; it is a powerful reality in the history of nations; it is a "world power" in contemporary history. Let us take hope for the victory of Christ in our country too. St John said:

This is the victory that overcomes the world, our faith (1 John 5:4).

We read in the gospels about a certain village that Jesus visited but did not work many miracles there because of their lack of faith.

Elsewhere we find from the lips of the Master the words:

I tell you solemnly, if your faith were the size of a mustard seed you could say to this mountain, "move from here to there", and it would move; nothing would be impossible for you (Matthew 17:20).

Faith in Jesus Christ is the greatest need of our country at this time. Only that faith can move the mountains of prejudice and the barriers of bigotry that keep our communities apart. The heart of the saving work of Jesus was reconciliation; reconciliation of men and women with God and reconciliation of men and women with one another. The most insuperable barriers in the time and culture of Jesus were those dividing Jew and Gentile and those dividing Jew and Samaritan. Both of these are dramatically abolished by the death and resurrection of Jesus Christ and the work of his Holy Spirit.

The removal of barriers of hostility between Jew and Samaritan seems to me to have remarkable relevance to our situation here. The Samaritans had broken away from both the religious and the political unity of the Jewish nation, and were despised, excluded, avoided and even hated on both counts. Relations between the Samaritans and the Jews were always tense; and each territory was unfriendly and sometimes dangerous to visitors or intruders from the other. Tensions heightened around the times of the great religious and national feasts of the respective communities. Periodic outbursts of communal violence marked the relationships between them. One does not need to point to parallels with our local situation.

Jesus was familiar with these tensions and from time to time had personal experience of them. Whenever he and his disciples planned to go up to Jerusalem to celebrate the great feasts, their shortest route lay through Samaria. On one of these occasions, we read that they passed along the borders of Samaria but not across it (cf. Luke 17:11); obviously communal tensions at that time were running high and a Jew would not have been safe in Samaritan territory. Instead they would have taken the much longer route down the Jordan valley and up to Jerusalem through Jericho.

Another time, as they were in fact passing through Samaria on the way to Jerusalem for Jesus' last Passover, a delegation from a Samaritan village refused to allow them to pass through their village. James and John, hot-tempered Jewish nationalists to whom Jesus had given the nickname, Boanerges, "the thunder boys", wanted to call down lightning from heaven to "burn them out of it". Jesus rebuked them: "You do not know of what spirit you are" (Luke 9:51–6).

The story has a remarkable sequel recounted in the Acts of the Apostles. After Pentecost, while the first Christians were dispersed from Judaea by persecution, Philip went to Samaria and "proclaimed the Christ" to a Samaritan village. We read that they "united in welcoming the message" and that as a result "there was great rejoicing in the town" (Acts

8:4–8). I like to think that it may have been the very same village which the two hardliners earlier had wanted to "firebomb". Love is stronger than fire. Love conquers hate and drives out fear.

The word "Samaritan" in Jesus' time was never used by Jews except as a term of abuse and contempt. Once angry Jews said of Jesus, "You are a Samaritan and possessed by a devil" (John 8:48). Jesus however never used the term "Samaritan" except as a term of praise and admiration. He regularly singled out Samaritans as examples of piety, gratitude and charity, holding them up to the Jews as models to imitate. Down all the Christian centuries, the term "Samaritan", once an expression of loathing, has been a synonym for charity and goodness. Jesus changed the use of words by radically transforming the relationship between Jews and Samaritans, making the two divided peoples into one "new creation" in Christ (2 Corinthians 2:17).

Similarly, the still vaster gulf between Jews and pagans is abolished by Jesus Christ; for, as St Paul says:

> He is the peace between us and he has made the two into one and broken down the barrier which used to keep them apart, actually destroying in his own person the hostility (Ephesians 2:14–15).

The power of Jesus Christ to make peace and to unite is not lesser now. May our faith be to the measure of his power. "The Troubles" are a testing time for our faith; but faith is made for testing and the test can purify and strengthen faith like iron smelted in a furnace.

It has been said:

> We do not know what the future holds, but we do know who holds the future.

With St Paul we who know that Jesus is Lord can say:

> I know who it is that I have put my trust in and I have no
> doubt at all that he is able to take care of all that I have
> entrusted to him until that Day (2 Timothy 1:12).

In the midst of our Troubles, we can lift up our hearts and say:

> We are the Easter people, and Alleluia is our song.